Introduction

Welcome to "The Israeli Passover Haggadah" – a celebration of tradition, faith, and the enduring spirit of Israel. Each year, as we gather together with family and friends around the Seder table, we reconnect with our rich Jewish heritage and bask in the togetherness of Jewish life. With this Haggadah, take Passover one step further by embracing the rich, vibrant tapestry of Israeli culture.

In this unique Haggadah, we blend timeless tradition with the modern narrative of Israel – the homeland of the Jewish people and a beacon of hope and innovation. Through captivating Israeli success stories, recipes for classic Israeli dishes, and modern Israeli slang, spend this Seder night embracing a deeper connection to your heritage – both ancient and modern.

Throughout the pages, you will encounter all the familiar passages of the Haggadah alongside illuminating insights into Israel's contributions to the world – from technological innovations and cultural significance to humanitarian endeavors and artistic achievements.

The English transliteration will always appear parallel to the original Hebrew text, with the English translation following below.

Also, icons alongside the text will help orient you and clarify what needs to be done next:

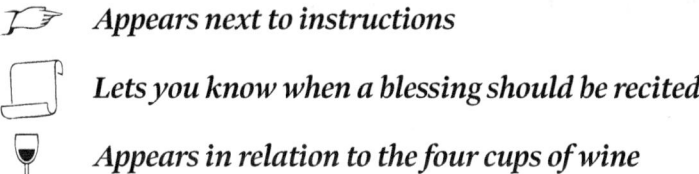

Appears next to instructions

Lets you know when a blessing should be recited

Appears in relation to the four cups of wine

You can find all of your favorite Passover songs (Chad Gadya, Who Knows One?, Go Down Moses, Eliyahu Ha-Navi) all together in the Songs chapter, so you can skip back and forth and incorporate them in your Seder as you go along.

Chag Sameach, and Am Yisrael Chai!

The Order of the Seder

6	**Kadesh**	— Blessing on the Wine
12	**Urchatz**	— Washing Hands
14	Israel in Technology	
16	**Karpas**	— The Leafy Vegetable
18	**Yachatz**	— Breaking the Middle Matzah
20	Israel in Science	
22	**Magid**	— Telling the Story of Exodus
28	Israel in Humanitarian Aid	
42	Israel in Art & Literature	
58	Israel in Medicine	
60	**Rachtzah**	— Washing Hands (this time, with a blessing)
62	**Motzi-Matzah**	— Blessing on the Matzah
63	Israel in Entertainment	
66	**Maror**	— Bitter Herb
68	**Korech**	— Maror Wrapped in Matzah
70	**Shulchan-Orech**	— The Festive Meal
72	Israel in Entrepreneurship	
74	**Tzafun**	— The Afikoman
76	**Barech**	— Blessing After the Meal
30	**Hallel**	— Praise to G-d
84	Israel in Sports	
86	**Nirtzah**	— Conclusion of the Seder
88	Songs	
98	Appendix – Israeli Recipes	

The Seder Plate

Zero'a
typically a lamb shank bone, often substituted for cooked chicken

Maror
a bitter vegetable, usually horseradish or lettuce

Beitzah
a hard-boiled egg

Charoset
a sweet paste made with apples and nuts

Karpas
a green leafy vegetable, usually parsley or celery

Hazeret
more of the same or a different bitter vegetable

Matzah
beside the seder plate, we place three whole matzahs, which will play an important part in the seder

Kadesh

קַדֵּשׁ

Blessing
on the Wine

Pour everyone a first full cup of wine.

 Recite the Kiddush blessing, adding the parentheses when the Seder falls on the Sabbath:

וַיְהִי עֶרֶב וַיְהִי בֹקֶר יוֹם הַשִּׁשִּׁי וַיְכֻלּוּ הַשָּׁמַיִם וְהָאָרֶץ וְכָל צְבָאָם. וַיְכַל אֱלֹהִים בַּיּוֹם הַשְּׁבִיעִי מְלַאכְתּוֹ אֲשֶׁר עָשָׂה וַיִּשְׁבֹּת בַּיּוֹם הַשְּׁבִיעִי מִכָּל מְלַאכְתּוֹ אֲשֶׁר עָשָׂה. וַיְבָרֶךְ אֱלֹהִים אֶת יוֹם הַשְּׁבִיעִי וַיְקַדֵּשׁ אוֹתוֹ כִּי בוֹ שָׁבַת מִכָּל מְלַאכְתּוֹ אֲשֶׁר בָּרָא אֱלֹהִים לַעֲשׂוֹת.

Vayehi erev, vayehi voker, yom ha-shishi. V'yechulu ha-shamayim v'ha'aretz v'chol tzeva'am. V'yechal Elohim ba-yom ha-shevi'i mi-kol melachto asher asah, v'yishbot ba-yom ha-shvi'i mi-kol melachto asher asah. V'yevarech Elohim et yom ha-shvi'i v'yekadesh oto, ki vo shavat mi-kol melachto asher bara Elohim la'asot.

And so it was evening, and so it was morning, the sixth day. And G-d had completed the skies and the earth and all their host. And on the seventh day, G-d finished His work which He had done, and on the seventh day G-d rested from the work which He had done. And G-d blessed the seventh day and sanctified it, for on that day He rested from His work and all that He had done.

בָּרוּךְ אַתָּה יְיָ אֱלֹהֵינוּ מֶלֶךְ הָעוֹלָם בּוֹרֵא פְּרִי הַגָּפֶן.

Baruch atah Adonai, Eloheinu melech ha-olam, borei peri ha-gafen.

Blessed are You, Lord our G-d, King of the universe, creator of the fruit of the vine.

בָּרוּךְ אַתָּה יְיָ אֱלֹהֵינוּ מֶלֶךְ הָעוֹלָם, אֲשֶׁר בָּחַר בָּנוּ מִכָּל עָם וְרוֹמְמָנוּ מִכָּל לָשׁוֹן וְקִדְּשָׁנוּ בְּמִצְוֹתָיו. וַתִּתֶּן לָנוּ יְיָ אֱלֹהֵינוּ בְּאַהֲבָה (בְּשַׁבָּת: שַׁבָּתוֹת לִמְנוּחָה וּ) מוֹעֲדִים לְשִׂמְחָה, חַגִּים וּזְמַנִּים לְשָׂשׂוֹן, אֶת יוֹם (הַשַּׁבָּת הַזֶּה וְאֶת יוֹם) חַג הַמַּצּוֹת הַזֶּה, זְמַן חֵרוּתֵנוּ (בְּאַהֲבָה), מִקְרָא קֹדֶשׁ, זֵכֶר לִיצִיאַת מִצְרָיִם. כִּי בָנוּ בָחַרְתָּ וְאוֹתָנוּ קִדַּשְׁתָּ מִכָּל הָעַמִּים, (וְשַׁבָּת) וּמוֹעֲדֵי קָדְשֶׁךָ (בְּאַהֲבָה וּבְרָצוֹן,) בְּשִׂמְחָה וּבְשָׂשׂוֹן הִנְחַלְתָּנוּ. בָּרוּךְ אַתָּה יְיָ, מְקַדֵּשׁ (הַשַּׁבָּת וְ)יִשְׂרָאֵל וְהַזְּמַנִּים.

Baruch atah Adonai, Eloheinu melech ha-olam, asher bachar banu mi-kol 'am v'romemanu mi-kol lashon v'kideshanu b'mitzvotav. V'titen lanu Adonai Eloheinu b'ahava (shabbatot li-mnucha v') mo'adim l'-simcha, chagim uzmanim l'sason, et yom (ha-shabbat hazeh ve'et yom) chag ha-matzot hazeh, zman cheruteinu (b'ahava) mikra kodesh, Zecher l'yetziyat mitzrayim. Ki banu bacharta v'otanu kidashta mi-kol ha-amim, (v'shabbat) umo'adei kodshecha (b'ahava uvratzon,) b'simcha uvsason hinchaltanu. Baruch atah Adonai, mekadesh (ha-shabbat v') Yisrael v'ha-zmanim.

Blessed are you, Lord our G-d, King of the universe, who has chosen us among all people and raised us above all languages, and sanctified us through His commandments. The Lord our G-d has lovingly given us (the Shabbat to rest, and) festivals to be joyful, holidays and special times for gladness, this (Shabbat day and this) Passover, our time of (loving) freedom, in holiness and in memory of the Exodus from Egypt. For us You have chosen and us You have sanctified from all the people, and You have (lovingly and willingly) given us (Shabbat and) the holy times for happiness and joy. Blessed are You, G-d, who sanctifies (the Shabbat and) the people of Israel and the festivities.

חי/ה בסרט   *Chai/a b'seret*

Literally: Hebrew for "living in a movie".

Meaning: used to describe someone with unrealistic expectations.

"If he thinks I'm going out in this rain, he's really *chai b'seret*."

On Saturday evening, add:

בָּרוּךְ אַתָּה יְיָ אֱלֹהֵינוּ מֶלֶךְ הָעוֹלָם, בּוֹרֵא מְאוֹרֵי הָאֵשׁ.

Baruch atah Adonai, Eloheinu melech ha-olam, borei me'orei ha-esh.

Blessed are You, Lord our G-d, King of the universe, creator of the light of fire.

בָּרוּךְ אַתָּה יְיָ אֱלֹהֵינוּ מֶלֶךְ הָעוֹלָם הַמַּבְדִּיל בֵּין קֹדֶשׁ לְחֹל, בֵּין אוֹר לְחֹשֶׁךְ, בֵּין יִשְׂרָאֵל לָעַמִּים, בֵּין יוֹם הַשְּׁבִיעִי לְשֵׁשֶׁת יְמֵי הַמַּעֲשֶׂה. בֵּין קְדֻשַּׁת שַׁבָּת לִקְדֻשַּׁת יוֹם טוֹב הִבְדַּלְתָּ, וְאֶת יוֹם הַשְּׁבִיעִי מִשֵּׁשֶׁת יְמֵי הַמַּעֲשֶׂה קִדַּשְׁתָּ. הִבְדַּלְתָּ וְקִדַּשְׁתָּ אֶת עַמְּךָ יִשְׂרָאֵל בִּקְדֻשָּׁתֶךָ. בָּרוּךְ אַתָּה יְיָ הַמַּבְדִּיל בֵּין קֹדֶשׁ לְקֹדֶשׁ.

Baruch atah Adonai, Eloheinu melech ha-olam, ha-mavdil beyn kodesh le-chol, beyn or le-choshech, beyn Israel l'amim, beyn yom ha-shvi'i l'sheshet yemey ha-ma'aseh. Beyn kedushat shabbat l'kedushat yom tov hivdalta, v'et yom ha-shvi'i mi-sheshet yemey ha-ma'aseh kidashta. Hivdalta v'kidashta et amcha Yisrael b'kdushatcha. Baruch atah Adonai ha-mavdil beyn kodesh l'kodesh.

Blessed are You, Lord our G-d, King of the universe, who makes a distinction between the holy and the profane, between light and darkness, between the people of Israel and the nations, between the seventh day and the six days of work. You have made the distinction between the sanctity of Shabbat and the sanctity of the holy day, and sanctified the seventh day of the six days of work. You have set apart and sanctified Your people of Israel with Your holiness. Blessed are You, G-d, who differentiates between the holy and the holy.

On the first Seder night, add:

בָּרוּךְ אַתָּה יְיָ אֱלֹהֵינוּ מֶלֶךְ הָעוֹלָם, שֶׁהֶחֱיָנוּ וְקִיְּמָנוּ וְהִגִּיעָנוּ לַזְּמַן הַזֶּה.

Baruch atah Adonai, Eloheinu melech ha-olam, sh'hecheyanu v'kiyemanu v'higiyanu l'zman hazeh.

Blessed are You, Lord our G-d, King of the universe, who has given us life, sustained us, and allowed us to reach this time.

Drink the first cup of wine.

תכלס **Tachles**

Literally: Yiddish for "purpose".

Meaning: bottom line, or "in reality".

"I know I said I would go study with her, but *tachles*, I'd rather stay at home."

Urchatz

וּרְחַץ

Washing Hands

☞ Wash your hands using a washing cup, pouring water three times onto each hand. Do not recite a blessing.

אחלה *Achla*

Literally: Arabic for "sweet" or "good".

Meaning: great, excellent, alright!

"I booked us a reservation for 7." "*Achla!*"

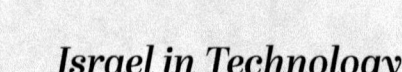

Israel in Technology

Astronaut Ilan Ramon

Ilan Ramon began his flying career in the Israeli Air Force when he graduated from the prestigious fighter pilot training course. He rose in the ranks to colonel, serving through many of Israel's wars and participating in Operation Opera, which saw Iraq's nuclear reactor destroyed.

NASA later selected Ramon to participate in the Columbia space shuttle missions, for which he trained for five long years to become the very first Israeli astronaut.

Tragically, Ramon was killed just minutes before landing back to Earth upon completion of his first space mission. His legacy as the first Israeli to go to space stays strong, and his determination and perseverance are an inspiration to many.

BabySense Monitor

Parents everywhere in the world are preoccupied with their children's safety. This is why Israeli company Hisense developed the BabySense monitor – a highly sensitive, contactless monitor that tracks baby's breathing and helps prevent the terrifying Sudden Infant Death Syndrome – a leading cause of infant fatality.

BabySense has sold millions of monitors around the world and helps babies – and their parents – breathe easy every single day.

Mobileye

Mobileye Technologies is revolutionizing the field of automobile security with its simple yet effective driver-assistance systems and autonomous driving technologies.

Focused on safety for motorists and pedestrians, Mobileye's systems are incorporated into millions of cars worldwide and have been adopted and endorsed by BMW, Volkswagen, and many more.

In 2017, Intel acquired Mobileye for $15.3 billion – at the time, the most expensive acquisition of an Israeli company and a groundbreaking step for the world of Israeli hi-tech.

Iron Dome

Constantly focused on the safety of its civilians, Israel pours significant funds and efforts into developing defensive military measures. Perhaps the most influential of these is the Iron Dome, an automatically deployed air defense system, which, for over a decade, has successfully intercepted thousands upon thousands of rockets, protecting Israeli towns and civilians from harm.

Backed and supported by the United States, Israel continues to tweak and perfect the Iron Dome system, promising security to every one of its people for as long as there are enemies that pose a threat.

USB Flash Drive

In the 1990s, when the World Wide Web and computing were still in their infancy and digital information was no simple thing to share, Israeli company M-Systems made history when they came up with the simple but genius solution of the disk-on-key – more commonly known as the USB flash drive.

Compact and user-friendly, the flash drive was ahead of its time in the classic style of Israeli technological innovation. Since then, it has inspired and born many more advanced solutions for storing and sharing digital data – making it an actual turning point in history.

Karpas

כַּרְפַּס

The Leafy Vegetable

☞ Take some karpas (parsley, celery, or another leafy green vegetable) and dip it into salt water.

📜 Recite the blessing:

בָּרוּךְ אַתָּה יְיָ אֱלֹהֵינוּ מֶלֶךְ הָעוֹלָם, בּוֹרֵא פְּרִי הָאֲדָמָה.

Baruch atah Adonai, Eloheinu Melech ha-olam, borei peri ha-adama.

Blessed are You, Lord our G-d, King of the universe, creator of the fruit of the earth.

☞ After reciting the blessing, eat the karpas.

בלגן *Balagan*

Literally: originally Persian for "attic".

Meaning: hot mess.

"Wow, you'd better clean up, your room is such a *balagan*."

Yachatz

יַחַץ

Breaking
the Middle Matzah

☞ Of the three matzahs we put aside at the start of the Seder, take the middle one and break it into two. Don't try to break it perfectly in half, as we want to have one piece bigger than the other.

☞ Take the larger piece and set it aside. This will be our Afikoman. It is customary for the leader of the seder to hide the Afikoman during the Seder for younger participants to find.

☞ Return the smaller piece to its place between the first and third matzahs.

טיל *Til*

Literally: Hebrew for "rocket".

Meaning: sounds good, excellent.

"Be ready at 8, I'll pick you up at home." "*Til.*"

Israel in Science

Nobel Laureate Daniel Kahneman

The 2002 Nobel Memorial Prize in Economic Sciences was awarded to Dr. Daniel Kahneman, an Israeli-American psychologist and economist. Known primarily for his innovative research into human judgment and decision-making, Kahneman grew up in Nazi-occupied France and immigrated to Israel when the young country was established in 1948.

Kahneman's cognitive theories about how we think and act have produced multiple academic papers and several books, which educate and enrich readers in various languages every day.

Invention of the Cherry Tomato

The cherry tomato is the perfect addition to any salad, sandwich, or casserole. Cute and sweet, it's hard to imagine a time without them.

In fact, cherry tomatoes are just one more of Israel's agricultural successes – they were invented in the Hebrew University's agricultural department in the city of Rehovot, following a long, 12-year breeding program.

Cherry tomatoes are widely popular in Israel and, of course, in the world. They make the perfect addition to a classic Israel breakfast, which usually includes an omelet, bread, and fresh vegetables on the side.

Decoding the Ribosome

Another Israeli honored to have received the Nobel Prize, this time in chemistry, is the esteemed scientist Ada Yonath. Together with her research partners, Yonath contributed to our modern understanding of the ribosome, a cellular structure responsible for translating genetic matter into proteins.

Yonath was the first woman in 45 years to win the Nobel Prize in chemistry, and her research and findings have fueled multiple scientific and medical discoveries, making her a true trailblazer of scientific curiosity and progress.

MyHeritage

The MyHeritage DNA testing platform gained popularity in the early 2000s when people discovered the helpful genealogy tool, which can help you determine your cultural heritage and even locate family members.

Founded and headquartered in Israel, MyHeritage has tens of millions of registered users whose genealogical information is shared on the website. The platform allows people, families, and entire cultures to learn and preserve their histories, bringing recognition to third-world societies and reuniting long-lost families.

Netafim Irrigation Systems

Being an agricultural state, Israeli technology is at the forefront of water and crop management solutions. One of these such solutions is Netafim Irrigation Systems, which pioneered drip irrigation technology for effective and efficient use of water and sustainable agriculture.

Netafim is involved in multiple sustainability projects all over the globe and works hard to make the world a more sustainable, green place for us all.

Magid

מַגִּיד

Telling the Story of Exodus

Uncover the Matzah for all to see, and raise it in the air while reciting the following:

הָא לַחְמָא עַנְיָא דִי אֲכָלוּ אַבְהָתָנָא בְּאַרְעָא דְמִצְרָיִם. כָּל דִכְפִין יֵיתֵי וְיֵיכֹל, כָּל דִצְרִיךְ יֵיתֵי וְיִפְסַח. הָשַׁתָּא הָכָא, לְשָׁנָה הַבָּאָה בְּאַרְעָא דְיִשְׂרָאֵל. הָשַׁתָּא עַבְדֵי, לְשָׁנָה הַבָּאָה בְּנֵי חוֹרִין.

Ha lachma anya, di achalu avhatana b'ar'a d'mitsrayim. Kol dichfin yetey v'yechol, kol ditsrich yetey v'yifsach. Hashata hacha, l'shana haba'a b'ara d'yisrael. Hashata avdey, l'shana haba'a bney chorin.

This is the bread of poverty that our ancestors ate in the land of Egypt. All who are hungry may come and eat, all who are in need may come and celebrate with us. Now we are here, here's to next year in the land of Israel. Now we are slaves, here's to next year as a free people.

 Put the matzah down and cover it again.

 Pour the second cup of wine.

Mah Nishtanah – What Is Different?

☞ It is traditional for the youngest participant of each Seder to ask the four questions, with the rest of the participants replying.

מַה נִּשְׁתַּנָּה הַלַּיְלָה הַזֶּה מִכָּל הַלֵּילוֹת ?
שֶׁבְּכָל הַלֵּילוֹת אָנוּ אוֹכְלִין חָמֵץ וּמַצָּה, הַלַּיְלָה הַזֶּה - כֻּלּוֹ מַצָּה.

שֶׁבְּכָל הַלֵּילוֹת אָנוּ אוֹכְלִין שְׁאָר יְרָקוֹת, - הַלַּיְלָה הַזֶּה מָרוֹר.

שֶׁבְּכָל הַלֵּילוֹת אֵין אָנוּ מַטְבִּילִין אֲפִילוּ פַּעַם אֶחָת, - הַלַּיְלָה הַזֶּה שְׁתֵּי פְעָמִים.

שֶׁבְּכָל הַלֵּילוֹת אָנוּ אוֹכְלִין בֵּין יוֹשְׁבִין וּבֵין מְסֻבִּין, - הַלַּיְלָה הַזֶּה כֻּלָּנוּ מְסֻבִּין.

Mah nishtanah halaylah hazeh mikol haleylot?

She-b'kol haleylot anu ochlin chametz u'matzah, halaylah hazeh – kulo matzah.

She-b'kol haleylot anu ochlin she'ar yerakot, halaylah hazeh – maror.

She-b'kol haleylot eyn anu matbilin afilu pa'am achat, halaylah hazeh – shtey pe'amim.

She-b'kol haleylot anu ochlin beynyoshvin u'beyn mesubin, halaylah hazeh – kulanu mesubin.

What makes this night different from any other night?

On every other night we eat chametz and matzah. On this night – only matzah.

On every other night we eat all kinds of vegetables. On this night – only maror.

On every other night we do not dip our vegetables even once. On this night – we dip twice.

Magid

On every other night we eat reclining and sitting straight. On this night – we all recline.

עֲבָדִים הָיִינוּ לְפַרְעֹה בְּמִצְרָיִם, וַיּוֹצִיאֵנוּ יְיָ אֱלֹהֵינוּ מִשָּׁם בְּיָד חֲזָקָה וּבִזְרוֹעַ נְטוּיָה. וְאִלּוּ לֹא הוֹצִיא הַקָּדוֹשׁ בָּרוּךְ הוּא אֶת אֲבוֹתֵינוּ מִמִּצְרַיִם, הֲרֵי אָנוּ וּבָנֵינוּ וּבְנֵי בָנֵינוּ מְשֻׁעְבָּדִים הָיִינוּ לְפַרְעֹה בְּמִצְרָיִם.

Avadim hayinu l'paroh b'mitsrayim, v'yotsi'anu Adonai Eloheinu misham b'yad chazakah u'vizro'a netuya. V'ilu lo hotzi ha-Kadosh Baruch Hu et avoteynu m'mitsrayim, harey anu u'vaneynu u'vney vaneynu meshu'abadim hayinu l'paroh b'mitsrayim

We were slaves of Pharoah in Egypt, until the Lord our G-d took us out from there with a strong hand and an outstretched arm. Had G-d, blessed be His name, not liberated our ancestors from Egypt, we and our sons and daughters and their sons and daughters would still be enslaved to Pharoah in Egypt today.

אֲפִילוּ כֻּלָּנוּ חֲכָמִים, כֻּלָּנוּ נְבוֹנִים, כֻּלָּנוּ זְקֵנִים, כֻּלָּנוּ יוֹדְעִים אֶת הַתּוֹרָה, מִצְוָה עָלֵינוּ לְסַפֵּר בִּיצִיאַת מִצְרָיִם. וְכָל הַמַּרְבֶּה לְסַפֵּר בִּיצִיאַת מִצְרַיִם הֲרֵי זֶה מְשֻׁבָּח.

V'afilu kulanu chachamim, kulanu nevonim, kulanu zkenim, kulanu yod'im et ha-torah, mitzvah aleynu lesaper b'yetsiat mitsrayim. V'chol hamarbeh lesaper b'yetsiat mitsrayim, harey zeh meshubach.

And although we are all intelligent, wise, learned, we all know the torah, we are commanded to tell the story of the Exodus from Egypt. And the more we tell the story, the better.

סוֹף סוֹף *Sof sof*

Literally: Hebrew for "end end".

Meaning: finally.

"Did you hear they got engaged?"
"*Sof sof*, it's been ten years!"

Magid

מַעֲשֶׂה בְּרַבִּי אֱלִיעֶזֶר וְרַבִּי יְהוֹשֻׁעַ וְרַבִּי אֶלְעָזָר בֶּן עֲזַרְיָה וְרַבִּי עֲקִיבָא וְרַבִּי טַרְפוֹן שֶׁהָיוּ מְסֻבִּין בִּבְנֵי בְרַק, וְהָיוּ מְסַפְּרִים בִּיצִיאַת מִצְרַיִם כָּל אוֹתוֹ הַלַּיְלָה עַד שֶׁבָּאוּ תַלְמִידֵיהֶם וְאָמְרוּ לָהֶם: רַבּוֹתֵינוּ, הִגִּיעַ זְמַן קְרִיאַת שְׁמַע שֶׁל שַׁחֲרִית.

Ma'aseh b'rabi Eliezer v'rabi Yehoshua v'rabi Elazar ben azaryah v'rabi akiva v'rabi tardon she-hayu mesubin bivney beraq, v'hayu mesaprim b'yetzi'at mitzrayim kol oto ha'laylah ad she-ba'u talmid-eyhem v'amru lahem: raboteynu, higiya zeman kriyat shema shel shacharit.

A story is told of Rabbi Eliezer and Rabbi Yehoshua and Rabbi Elazar Ben Azaryah and Rabbi Akiva and Rabbk Tarfon, who resided in Benei Beraq, and told the story of the exodus from Egypt all that night. Until their students came to them and told them: our teachers, it is time to say the shema for the morning prayer.

Ma pit'om מה פתאום

Literally: Hebrew for "what is this suddenly?"

Meaning: no way, you have to be kidding.

"So I hear you're great at Hebrew!"
"*Ma pitom*, I can't read to save my life!"

Israel in Humanitarian Aid

IsraAID

IsraAid is an Israeli non-governmental organization (NGO) renowned for its humanitarian efforts in responding to global crises and disasters. Founded in 2001, IsraAid operates in various regions around the world, providing emergency relief, medical assistance, and long-term support to communities affected by conflict, natural disasters, and other challenges.

Over the years, IsraAid has responded to numerous humanitarian crises, including providing aid to refugees fleeing conflict, supporting communities affected by earthquakes and tsunamis, and assisting in recovery efforts after hurricanes and other natural disasters.

Through its commitment to humanitarian values and impactful interventions, IsraAid continues to make a meaningful difference in the lives of those facing adversity, embodying the spirit of Jewish solidarity and compassion.

Innovation: Africa

Israel excels in the field of solar and water technologies, and Israeli non-profit organization Innovation: Africa aspires to harness these solutions to bring sustainable living to rural African communities.

The organization provides reliable electricity for lighting, refrigeration, and powering essential medical equipment, while also improving access to clean water for drinking, irrigation, and sanitation. Its incredible initiatives have positively impacted for the better the lives of millions of people.

Israeli Flying Aid

Israeli Flying Aid (IFA) is an Israeli non-profit organization dedicated to providing humanitarian aid and disaster relief to communities around the world. Founded in 2005 by Gal Lusky, IFA operates on the principles of volunteerism, compassion, and solidarity.

What sets IFA apart is its commitment to impartial humanitarianism, extending aid to people regardless of their nationality, ethnicity, or religion. The organization has responded to crises in various countries, including Haiti, the Philippines, Nepal, Syria, and more. Israeli Flying Aid exemplifies Israel's commitment to humanitarian values and its willingness to extend assistance to those in need, regardless of geopolitical considerations.

Save a Child's Heart

In 1995, Dr. Ami Cohen founded Save a Child's Heart – an Israeli non-profit organization dedicated to providing life-saving cardiac care to children from developing countries.

Running on volunteer medical professionals, SACH provides advanced cardiac care, including surgeries, catheterizations, and post-operative care, extending its reach to thousands of children worldwide in need of life-saving medical care.

The Four Children

כְּנֶגֶד אַרְבָּעָה בָנִים דִּבְּרָה תוֹרָה. אֶחָד חָכָם, וְאֶחָד רָשָׁע, וְאֶחָד תָּם, וְאֶחָד שֶׁאֵינוֹ יוֹדֵעַ לִשְׁאוֹל.

Ke-neged arba'ah banim dibrah torah. Echad chacham, v'echad rasha, v'echad tam, v'eched she'eyno yode'a lishol.

The Torah tells us of four children. One who is wise, one who is wicked, one who is simple, and one who does not know how to ask.

Magid

חָכָם מָה הוּא אוֹמֵר?
מה הָעֵדוֹת וְהַחֻקִּים וְהַמִשְׁפָּטִים אֲשֶׁר צִוָּה יְיָ אֱלֹהֵינוּ אֶתְכֶם?
וְאַף אַתָּה אֱמָר לוֹ כְּהִלְכוֹת הַפֶּסַח: אֵין מַפְטִירִין אַחַר הַפֶּסַח אֲפִיקוֹמָן.

Chacham ma hu omer?

Me ha-edot v'ha-hukim v'ha-mishpatim asher tsivah Adonai Eloheynu etchem?

V'af atah emor lo k'hilchot ha'pesach: eyn maftirin ahar ha-pesach afikoman.

The wise one, what does he say?

"What are these rules and rituals that the Lord our G-d has commanded you?"

And you shall tell him all about the rituals of Passover up until the very last rule, that we do not eat anything else after the Afikoman.

רָשָׁע מָה הוּא אוֹמֵר?
מָה הָעֲבֹדָה הַזֹּאת לָכֶם?
לָכֶם - וְלֹא לוֹ. וּלְפִי שֶׁהוֹצִיא אֶת עַצְמוֹ מִן הַכְּלָל כָּפַר בָּעִקָּר. וְאַף אַתָּה הַקְהֵה אֶת שִׁנָּיו וֶאֱמֹר לוֹ: בַּעֲבוּר זֶה עָשָׂה יְיָ לִי בְּצֵאתִי מִמִּצְרָיִם. לִי - וְלֹא לוֹ. אִלּוּ הָיָה שָׁם, לֹא הָיָה נִגְאָל.

Rasha ma hu omer?

Me ha'avoda hazot lachem?

Lachem- v'lo lo. U'lefi she-hotsi et atsmo min ha-klal kafar ba-ikar. V'af atah hakheh et shi-nav v'emor lo: ba'avur ze asah Adonai li b'tseyti m'mitsrayim. Li- v'lo lo. Ilu hayah sham, lo ha-yah nigal.

The wicked one, what does he say?

"What are these rules you follow?"

You – and not he. By excluding himself from his people, he denies the foundation of Passover. You shall tell him: It is because of what G-d did for me when I was liberated from Egypt. Me, and not him. Had he been there, he would not have been freed.

תָּם מָה הוּא אוֹמֵר?

מַה זֹּאת?

וְאָמַרְתָּ אֵלָיו: בְּחֹזֶק יָד הוֹצִיאָנוּ יְיָ מִמִּצְרַיִם, מִבֵּית עֲבָדִים.

Tam ma hu omer?

"Ma zot?"

V'amarta eylav: b'chozek yad hotzi'anu Adonai m'mitzrayim, mi-beyt avadim.

The simple one, what does he say?

"What's all this?"

And you shall say to him: G-d liberated us with a mighty hand from Egypt and from slavery.

וְשֶׁאֵינוֹ יוֹדֵעַ לִשְׁאוֹל - אַתְּ פְּתַח לוֹ, שֶׁנֶּאֱמַר: וְהִגַּדְתָּ לְבִנְךָ בַּיּוֹם הַהוּא לֵאמֹר, בַּעֲבוּר זֶה עָשָׂה יְיָ לִי בְּצֵאתִי מִמִּצְרָיִם.

V'she-eyno yode'a lishol – at petach lo, she-ne'emar: v'hi-gadla l'vincha be-yom hahu l'eymor, ba'avur ze asah Adonai li b'tsyeti m'mitsrayim.

And the one who does not know how to ask, you shall tell him the story yourself, as it is said: tell your child on that day, it is because of what G-d did for me when I came out of Egypt.

🚩 Raise your full cup of wine and say together:

וְהִיא שֶׁעָמְדָה לַאֲבוֹתֵינוּ וְלָנוּ. שֶׁלֹּא אֶחָד בִּלְבָד עָמַד עָלֵינוּ לְכַלּוֹתֵנוּ, אֶלָּא שֶׁבְּכָל דּוֹר וָדוֹר עוֹמְדִים עָלֵינוּ לְכַלּוֹתֵנוּ, וְהַקָּדוֹשׁ בָּרוּךְ הוּא מַצִּילֵנוּ מִיָּדָם.

V'hi she-amda l'avoteynu v'lanu.
She-lo echad bilvad amad aleynu l'chaloteinu, ela she-b'chol dor v'dor, omdim aleynu l'chaloteinu, v'ha-Kadosh Baruch Hu matsiley-nu m'yadam.

This promise has been upheld for our ancestors and for us.

For over the years, every generation, there have been those who have wanted to defeat and annihilate us, and G-d, Blessed be His Name, has saved us from them time and time again.

 Put down the cup of wine.

גמור/ה *Gamur/gmura*

Literally: Hebrew for "finished".

Meaning: tired, exhausted, spent.

"Wow, I just worked a 12-hour shift, I'm completely *gmura*."

בדוק *Baduk*

Literally: Hebrew for "confirmed", "verified".

Meaning: for sure.

"Do you want to come to this party with me?" "*Baduk!*"

The Ten Plagues

אֵלּוּ עֶשֶׂר מַכּוֹת שֶׁהֵבִיא הַקָּדוֹשׁ בָּרוּךְ הוּא עַל הַמִּצְרִים בְּמִצְרַיִם, וְאֵלּוּ הֵן:

Eylu eser ha-makot she-hevi ha-Kadosh Baruch Hu al ha-mitsrim b'mitsrayim, v'eylu hen:

These are the ten plagues that G-d, Blessed be His Name, brought down upon the Egyptians in Egypt:

 As you recite the ten plagues, pour a drop of wine from your cup onto a plate for each.

דָּם Dam **Blood**

צְפַרְדֵּעַ Tsfardeya **Frogs**

כִּנִּים Kinim **Lice**

עָרוֹב Arov **Wild Beasts**

Magid

דֶּבֶר Dever **Plague**

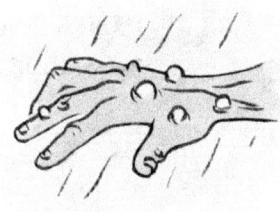

שְׁחִין Shechin **Boils**

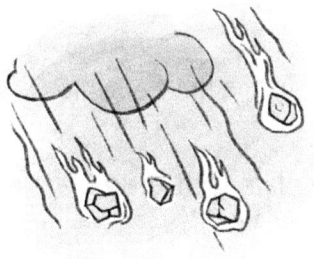

בָּרָד Barad **Hail**

אַרְבֶּה Arbeh **Locusts**

חֹשֶׁךְ Choshech **Darkness**

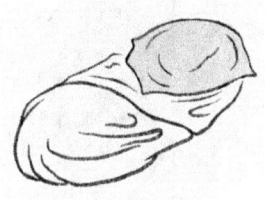

מַכַּת בְּכוֹרוֹת Makat Bechorot **Slaying of the Firstborn**

רַבִּי יְהוּדָה הָיָה נוֹתֵן בָּהֶם סִמָּנִים:

Rabi Yehudah hayah noten bahem simanim:

Rabbi Yehuda would assign them mnemonics:

דְּצַ"ךְ	Detsach (blood, frogs, lice)
עֲדַ"שׁ	Adash (wild beasts, plague, boils)
בְּאַחַ"ב	B'achav (hail, locusts, darkness, slaying of the firstborn)

 Pour another drop of wine for each of the three mnemonics.

 Remove the cup of wine and the plate with the wine you spilled and refill your second cup of wine.

Magid

רַבִּי יוֹסֵי הַגְּלִילִי אוֹמֵר: מִנַּיִן אַתָּה אוֹמֵר שֶׁלָּקוּ הַמִּצְרִים בְּמִצְרַיִם עֶשֶׂר מַכּוֹת וְעַל הַיָּם לָקוּ חֲמִשִּׁים מַכּוֹת?

בְּמִצְרַיִם מָה הוּא אוֹמֵר? וַיֹּאמְרוּ הַחַרְטֻמִּים אֶל פַּרְעֹה: אֶצְבַּע אֱלֹהִים הִוא, וְעַל הַיָּם מָה הוּא אוֹמֵר? וַיַּרְא יִשְׂרָאֵל אֶת הַיָּד הַגְּדֹלָה אֲשֶׁר עָשָׂה יְיָ בְּמִצְרַיִם, וַיִּירְאוּ הָעָם אֶת יְיָ, וַיַּאֲמִינוּ בַּיְיָ וּבְמֹשֶׁה עַבְדּוֹ. כַּמָּה לָקוּ בָּאֶצְבַּע? עֶשֶׂר מַכּוֹת. אֱמוֹר מֵעַתָּה: בְּמִצְרַיִם לָקוּ עֶשֶׂר מַכּוֹת וְעַל הַיָּם לָקוּ חֲמִשִּׁים מַכּוֹת.

Rabi Yosey ha-glili omer: mi-nay-in atah omer she-laku ha-mitz-rim b'mitzrayim eser makot v'al ha-yam laku chamishim makot?

B'mitzrayim ma hu omer? Va-yomru ha-chartumim el paroh: etsba Elohim hi, v'al ha-yam me hu omer? Va-yar Yisrael et ha-yad ha-gedolah asher asa Adonay b'mitsrayim, va-yiru ha-am et Adonay, va-ya'aminu b'Adonay u'v'moshe avdo. Kama laku v'etsba? Eser makot. Emor me'ata: b'mitsrayim laku eser makot v'al ha-yam laku chamishim makot.

Rabbi Yossey of the Galillei would ask: how do we know that the Egyptians were struck by ten plagues in Egypt and fifty plagues at sea?

In Egypt, what does it say? And the magicians said to Pharaoh: it is the hand of G-d. And at sea, what does it say? And Israel saw the mighty hand that G-d swept upon Egypt, and they feared G-d and trusted in Him and in Moses, his servant. Hoy many were they struck by the hand? Ten plagues. Thus, you shall say from now on: In Egypt they were struck by ten plagues and at sea they were struck by fifty plagues.

רַבִּי אֱלִיעֶזֶר אוֹמֵר: מִנַּיִן שֶׁכָּל מַכָּה וּמַכָּה שֶׁהֵבִיא הַקָּדוֹשׁ בָּרוּךְ הוּא עַל הַמִּצְרִים בְּמִצְרַיִם הָיְתָה שֶׁל אַרְבַּע מַכּוֹת?

שֶׁנֶּאֱמַר: יְשַׁלַּח בָּם חֲרוֹן אַפּוֹ, עֶבְרָה וָזַעַם וְצָרָה, מִשְׁלַחַת מַלְאֲכֵי רָעִים. עֶבְרָה – אַחַת, וָזַעַם – שְׁתַּיִם, וְצָרָה – שָׁלֹשׁ, מִשְׁלַחַת מַלְאֲכֵי רָעִים – אַרְבַּע. אֱמוֹר מֵעַתָּה: בְּמִצְרַיִם לָקוּ אַרְבָּעִים מַכּוֹת וְעַל הַיָּם לָקוּ מָאתַיִם מַכּוֹת.

Rabi Eliezer omer: mi-nayin she-kol makah v'makah she-hevi ha-Kadosh Baruch Hu al ha-mitsrim b'mitsrayim haytah shel arba makot?

She-ne'emar: yishlach bahem charon apo, evrah v'za'am v'tsarah, mishlachat mal'achei ra'im. Evra – achat, v'za'am – shtayim, v'tsarah – shalosh, mishlachat mal'achei ra'im – arba. Emor me-atah: b'mitsrayim laku arba'im makot v'al ha-yam laku matayim makot.

Rabbi Eliezer would ask: how do we know that each plague inflicted by G-d on the Egyptians in Egypt was worth four plagues?

It is said: and he unleashed upon them his rage, anger and wrath and troubles, a delegation of messengers of evil. Anger – is one, wrath – makes two, troubles – make three, and messengers of evil make four. Thus, you shall say from now on: In Egypt they were struck by forty plagues, and at sea they were struck by two hundred plagues.

Magid

רַבִּי עֲקִיבָא אוֹמֵר: מִנַּיִן שֶׁכָּל מַכָּה וּמַכָּה שֶׁהֵבִיא הַקָּדוֹשׁ בָּרוּךְ הוּא עַל הַמִּצְרִים בְּמִצְרַיִם הָיְתָה שֶׁל חָמֵשׁ מַכּוֹת?

שֶׁנֶּאֱמַר: יְשַׁלַּח בָּם חֲרוֹן אַפּוֹ, עֶבְרָה וָזַעַם וְצָרָה, מִשְׁלַחַת מַלְאֲכֵי רָעִים. חֲרוֹן אַפּוֹ - אַחַת, עֶבְרָה - שְׁתַּיִם, וָזַעַם - שָׁלֹשׁ, וְצָרָה - אַרְבַּע, מִשְׁלַחַת מַלְאֲכֵי רָעִים - חָמֵשׁ. אֱמֹר מֵעַתָּה: בְּמִצְרַיִם לָקוּ חֲמִשִּׁים מַכּוֹת וְעַל הַיָּם לָקוּ חֲמִשִּׁים וּמָאתַיִם מַכּוֹת.

Rabi Akiva omer: mi-nayin she-kol makah v'makah she-hevi ha-Kadosh Baruch Hu al ha-mitsrim b'mitsrayim hayta shel chamesh makot?

She-ne'emar: yishlach bam charon apo, evrah v'za'am v'tsarah, mishlachat mal'achei ra'im. Charon apo – achat, evra – shtayim, v'za'am – shalosh, v'tsarah – arba, mishlachat mal'achei ra'im – chamesh. Emor me-atah: b'mitsrayim laku chamishim makot v'al ha-yam laku chamishim u'matay-im makot.

Rabbi Akiva would ask: how do we know that each plague inflicted by G-d on the Egyptians in Egypt was worth five plagues?

It is said: and he unleashed upon them his rage, anger and wrath and troubles, a delegation of messengers of evil. Rage – is one, anger – makes two, wrath – makes three, troubles – make four, and messengers of evil make five. Thus, you shall say from now on: In Egypt they were struck by fifty plagues, and at sea they were struck by fifty and two hundred plagues.

Israel in Art & Literature

Designer Inbal Dror

You've seen her creations on red carpets all over the world, but you may not have known a talented Israeli designer was behind them. Inbal Dror, born and raised in Ashdod, Israel, built an empire of haute fashion that designs wedding gowns and evening wear for celebrities such as Beyoncé, Ivanka Trump, and Bar Refaeli.

Educated, married, and living in Israel with 75 worldwide boutique stores, Dror shows what it truly means to be an internationally successful Israeli.

Musician Itzhak Perlman

Itzhak Perlman is a world-renowned violinist born in Israel in 1945. Despite facing physical challenges due to polio at a young age, Perlman's exceptional talent and determination propelled him to become one of the most celebrated musicians of his generation.

Perlman's Israeli heritage is often reflected in his performances, showcasing a deep connection to his roots and a rich musical tradition. Throughout his illustrious career, he has not only captivated audiences with his unparalleled skill but has also served as a cultural ambassador, promoting Israeli music and fostering cross-cultural understanding through the universal language of music.

Artist Yaacov Agam

You may have seen his "Agamographs", uniquely colorful, geometrical works of art, exhibited in museums across the globe, but there is so much more to Israeli artist Yaacov Agam than just shape and color.

Throughout his career, Agam has explored various mediums, including painting, sculpture, and printmaking, pushing the boundaries of traditional artistic techniques and challenging perceptions of space and reality.

His dedication to breaking new ground and inspiring creativity has earned him international acclaim and numerous awards, solidifying his legacy as one of the most innovative and influential artists of the 20th century.

Yuval Noah Harari

Best known for his groundbreaking book "Sapiens: A Brief History of Humankind," Yuval Noah Harari is an Israeli historian and anthropologist whose thought-provoking work has garnered worldwide attention.

A modern-day Darwin, Harari delves into the complexities of human evolution. With his unique ability to blend history, anthropology, and philosophy, he offers profound insights into the past, present, and future of humanity.

Harari's influence extends beyond academia, as his ideas continue to shape global discourse on some of the most pressing issues of our time.

Dayeinu

כַּמָּה מַעֲלוֹת טוֹבוֹת לַמָּקוֹם עָלֵינוּ!

אִלּוּ הוֹצִיאָנוּ מִמִּצְרַיִם וְלֹא עָשָׂה בָהֶם שְׁפָטִים, דַּיֵּינוּ.

אִלּוּ עָשָׂה בָהֶם שְׁפָטִים, וְלֹא עָשָׂה בֵאלֹהֵיהֶם, דַּיֵּינוּ.

אִלּוּ עָשָׂה בֵאלֹהֵיהֶם, וְלֹא הָרַג אֶת בְּכוֹרֵיהֶם, דַּיֵּינוּ.

אִלּוּ הָרַג אֶת בְּכוֹרֵיהֶם וְלֹא נָתַן לָנוּ אֶת מָמוֹנָם, דַּיֵּינוּ.

אִלּוּ נָתַן לָנוּ אֶת מָמוֹנָם וְלֹא קָרַע לָנוּ אֶת הַיָּם, דַּיֵּינוּ.

אִלּוּ קָרַע לָנוּ אֶת הַיָּם וְלֹא הֶעֱבִירָנוּ בְתוֹכוֹ בֶּחָרָבָה, דַּיֵּינוּ.

אִלּוּ הֶעֱבִירָנוּ בְתוֹכוֹ בֶּחָרָבָה וְלֹא שִׁקַּע צָרֵנוּ בְּתוֹכוֹ, דַּיֵּינוּ.

אִלּוּ שִׁקַּע צָרֵנוּ בְּתוֹכוֹ וְלֹא סִפֵּק צָרְכֵּנוּ בַּמִּדְבָּר אַרְבָּעִים שָׁנָה, דַּיֵּינוּ.

אִלּוּ סִפֵּק צָרְכֵּנוּ בַּמִּדְבָּר אַרְבָּעִים שָׁנָה וְלֹא הֶאֱכִילָנוּ אֶת הַמָּן, דַּיֵּינוּ.

Kama ma'alot tovot la-makom aleynu!

Ilu hotsi'anu m'mitsrayim v'lo asah vahem shefatim, dayeinu.

Ilu asah behm shefatim v'lo asah b'eloheyhem, dayeinu.

Ilu asah b'eloheyhem v'lo harag et bechoreyhem, dayeinu.

Ilu harag et bechoreyhem v'lo natan lanu et mamonam, dayeinu.

Ilu natan lanu et mamonam v'lo kara lanu et hayam, dayeinu.

Ilu kara lanu et hayam v'lo he'eyviranu betocho b'charavah, dayeinu.

Ilu he'eyviranu betocho b'charavah v'lo shika tsareynu betocho, dayeinu.

Ilu shika tsareynu betocho v'lo sipek tsarcheynu ba-midbar arba'im shanah, dayeinu.

Ilu sipek tsarcheynu ba-midbar arba'im shanah v'lo he'eychilanu et ha-man, dayeinu.

Magid

Ilu he'eychilanu et ha-man v'lo natan lanu et ha-shabbat, dayeinu.	אִלּוּ הֶאֱכִילָנוּ אֶת הַמָּן וְלֹא נָתַן לָנוּ אֶת הַשַּׁבָּת, דַּיֵּנוּ.
Ilu natan lanu et ha-shabbat v'lo kervanu lifney har sinai, dayeinu.	אִלּוּ קֵרְבָנוּ לִפְנֵי הַר סִינַי, וְלֹא נָתַן לָנוּ אֶת הַתּוֹרָה, דַּיֵּנוּ.
Ilu kervanu lifney har sinai v'lo natan lanu et ha-torah, dayeinu.	אִלּוּ נָתַן לָנוּ אֶת הַשַּׁבָּת, וְלֹא קֵרְבָנוּ לִפְנֵי הַר סִינַי, דַּיֵּנוּ.
Ilu natan lanu et ha-torah v'lo hichnisanu l'eretz yisrael, dayeinu.	אִלּוּ נָתַן לָנוּ אֶת הַתּוֹרָה וְלֹא הִכְנִיסָנוּ לְאֶרֶץ יִשְׂרָאֵל, דַּיֵּנוּ.
Ilu hichnisanu l'eretz Yisrael v'lo vana lanu et beyt ha-behira, dayeinu.	אִלּוּ הִכְנִיסָנוּ לְאֶרֶץ יִשְׂרָאֵל וְלֹא בָנָה לָנוּ אֶת בֵּית הַבְּחִירָה, דַּיֵּנוּ.

How many good favors G-d has bestowed upon us!

Had He liberated us from Egypt and not carried out justice against the Egyptians, we would have been grateful enough.

Had He carried out justice against the Egyptians and not against their gods, we would have been grateful enough.

Had He carried out justice against their gods and not slain their first-borns, we would have been grateful enough.

Had He slain their firstborns and not given us their treasures, we would have been grateful enough.

Had He given us their treasures and not split the sea for us, we would have been grateful enough.

Had He split the sea for us and not let us through it on dry land, we would have been grateful enough.

Had He led us through the sea on dry land and not drowned our enemies in it, we would have been grateful enough.

Had He drowned our enemies in the sea and not provided for us in the desert for forty years, we would have been grateful enough.

Had He provided for us in the desert for forty years and not given us the manna, we would have been grateful enough.

Had He given us the manna and not given us the Sabbath, we would have been grateful enough.

Had He given us the Sabbath and not brought us to Mount Sinai, we would have been grateful enough.

Had He brought us to Mount Sinai and not given us the Torah, we would have been grateful enough.

Magid

Had He given us the Torah and not brought us into Israel, we would have been grateful enough.

Had He brought us into Israel and not built the Temple of worship, we would have been grateful enough.

עַל אַחַת, כַּמָּה וְכַמָּה, טוֹבָה כְפוּלָה וּמְכֻפֶּלֶת לַמָּקוֹם עָלֵינוּ: שֶׁהוֹצִיאָנוּ מִמִּצְרַיִם, וְעָשָׂה בָהֶם שְׁפָטִים, וְעָשָׂה בֵאלֹהֵיהֶם, וְהָרַג אֶת בְּכוֹרֵיהֶם, וְנָתַן לָנוּ אֶת מָמוֹנָם, וְקָרַע לָנוּ אֶת הַיָּם, וְהֶעֱבִירָנוּ בְתוֹכוֹ בֶּחָרָבָה, וְשִׁקַּע צָרֵנוּ בְּתוֹכוֹ, וְסִפֵּק צָרְכֵּנוּ בַּמִּדְבָּר אַרְבָּעִים שָׁנָה, וְהֶאֱכִילָנוּ אֶת הַמָּן, וְנָתַן לָנוּ אֶת הַשַּׁבָּת, וְקֵרְבָנוּ לִפְנֵי הַר סִינַי, וְנָתַן לָנוּ אֶת הַתּוֹרָה, וְהִכְנִיסָנוּ לְאֶרֶץ יִשְׂרָאֵל, וּבָנָה לָנוּ אֶת בֵּית הַבְּחִירָה לְכַפֵּר עַל כָּל עֲוֹנוֹתֵינוּ.

Al achat kama v'chama, tova kfula u'mechupelet la-makon aleynu. She-hotzi'anu mi-mitsrayim, v'asa beham shefatim, v'asa b'eloheyhem, v'harag et bechoryhem, v'natan lanu et mamonam, v'kara lanu et ha-yam, v'he'eviranu betocho b'charavah, v'shika tsareynu betocho, v'sipek tsarkeynu ba-midbar arba'im shanah, v'he'echilanu et ha-man, v'natan lanu et ha-shabat, v'kervanu lifney har sinai, v'natan lanu et ha-torah, v'hichnisanu l'eretz Yisrael, u'vana lanu et beyt ha-bechirah lechaper al kol avonoteynu.

How much good God gives us, which is doubled and tripled. He liberated us from Egypt, and carried out justice against the Egyptians, and carried out justice against their gods, and slayed their firstborns, and gave us their treasures, and split the sea for us, and led us through the sea on dry land, and drowned our enemies in the sea, and provided for us in the desert for forty years, and gave us the manna, and gave us the Sabbath, and brought us to Mount Sinai, and gave us the Torah, and brought us into Israel, and built the Temple of worship to atone for all of our sins.

The Symbols of Passover

רַבָּן גַּמְלִיאֵל הָיָה אוֹמֵר: כָּל שֶׁלֹּא אָמַר שְׁלֹשָׁה דְבָרִים אֵלּוּ בַּפֶּסַח, לֹא יָצָא יְדֵי חוֹבָתוֹ, וְאֵלּוּ הֵן:

Raban Gamilel hayah womer: kol she-lo amar ahloshah devarim eylu ba-pesach, lo yatsa yedey chovato, v'eylu hen:

Rabbi Gamliel would say, all who have not recited these three things on Passover have not done their duty. And these things are:

☞ All say together:

פֶּסַח, מַצָּה, וּמָרוֹר.

Pesach, matzah, u'maror.

Pesach, Matzah, and Bitter Herbs.

Magid

> ## נשמה *Neshama*
>
> Literally: Hebrew for "soul".
>
> Meaning: term of endearment, sometimes used ironically
>
> "*Neshama*, I know you're trying to park here, but I have to unload my stock first."

פֶּסַח שֶׁהָיוּ אֲבוֹתֵינוּ אוֹכְלִים בִּזְמַן שֶׁבֵּית הַמִּקְדָּשׁ הָיָה קַיָּם, עַל שׁוּם מָה?

עַל שׁוּם שֶׁפָּסַח הַקָּדוֹשׁ בָּרוּךְ הוּא עַל בָּתֵּי אֲבוֹתֵינוּ בְּמִצְרַיִם, שֶׁנֶּאֱמַר: וַאֲמַרְתֶּם זֶבַח פֶּסַח הוּא לַיי, אֲשֶׁר פָּסַח עַל בָּתֵּי בְנֵי יִשְׂרָאֵל בְּמִצְרַיִם בְּנָגְפּוֹ אֶת מִצְרַיִם, וְאֶת בָּתֵּינוּ הִצִּיל, וַיִּקֹּד הָעָם וַיִּשְׁתַּחֲווּ.

Pesach she-hayu avoteynu ochlim bizman she-beyt ha-mikdash hayah kayam, al shum mah?
Al shum she-pasach ha-Kadosh Baruch Hu al batey avoteynu b'mitsrayim, she-ne'emar: v'amartem zevach pesach hu l'Adonai, asher pasach al batey bney Yisrael b'mitsrayim b'nogfo et mitsrayim, v'et bateynu hitsil, vayikod ha'am vayishtachavu.

Pesach, the sacrificial offering that our ancestors would eat while the Temple was standing. What is the meaning of it?

In memory of how G-d passed over the homes of our ancestors in Egypt, sparing them. As it is said: The Pesach is an offering to G-d, who passed over the homes of the Israelites in Egypt as He smote the Egyptians and saved our homes. And the people bowed and genuflected before Him.

☞ **Raise the matzah and say:**

מַצָּה זוֹ שֶׁאָנוּ אוֹכְלִים, עַל שׁוּם מָה? עַל שׁוּם שֶׁלֹּא הִסְפִּיק בְּצֵקָם שֶׁל אֲבוֹתֵינוּ לְהַחֲמִיץ עַד שֶׁנִּגְלָה עֲלֵיהֶם מֶלֶךְ מַלְכֵי הַמְּלָכִים, הַקָּדוֹשׁ בָּרוּךְ הוּא, וּגְאָלָם, שֶׁנֶּאֱמַר: וַיֹּאפוּ אֶת הַבָּצֵק אֲשֶׁר הוֹצִיאוּ מִמִּצְרַיִם עֻגֹת מַצּוֹת, כִּי לֹא חָמֵץ, כִּי גֹרְשׁוּ מִמִּצְרַיִם וְלֹא יָכְלוּ לְהִתְמַהְמֵהַּ, וְגַם צֵדָה לֹא עָשׂוּ לָהֶם.

Matzah zo she-anu ochlim. Al shum mah?

Al shum she-lo hispik betsekam ahel avoteynu l'hachmitz ad she-niglah aleyhem Melech malchei ha-mlachim, Ha-Kadosh Baruch Hu, u'gealam, she-ne'emar: vayofu et ha-batsek asher hotsi'u m'mitsrayim ugot matzot, ki lo chametz, ki gorshu m'mitsrayim v'lo yachlu l'hit-mahamehah, v'gam tseydah lo asu lahem.

Matzah, this unleavened bread that we eat, what is the meaning of it?

In memory of the unleavened bread that our ancestors made and did not have time to rise before the King of Kings, G-d, Blessed be His Name, appeared before them and redeemed them. It is said: and they baked the dough that they brought with them from Egypt into matzahs, because it did not rise, as they were banished from Egypt and could not delay and did not even have time to prepare provisions.

Magid

☞ Raise the maror and say:

מָרוֹר זֶה שֶׁאָנוּ אוֹכְלִים, עַל שׁוּם מָה?
עַל שׁוּם שֶׁמֵּרְרוּ הַמִּצְרִים אֶת חַיֵּי אֲבוֹתֵינוּ בְּמִצְרַיִם, שֶׁנֶּאֱמַר: וַיְמָרֲרוּ אֶת חַיֵּיהֶם בַּעֲבֹדָה קָשָׁה, בְּחֹמֶר וּבִלְבֵנִים וּבְכָל עֲבֹדָה בַּשָּׂדֶה אֵת כָּל עֲבֹדָתָם אֲשֶׁר עָבְדוּ בָהֶם בְּפָרֶךְ

Maror ze she-anu ochlim, al shum mah?

Al shum she-mereyru ham-itsrim et chayey avoteinu b'mitsrayim, she-ne'emar: vayemareru et chayeyhem b'avoda kasha, b'chomer u'vil-venim u'vechol avoda ba-sa-deh et kol avodatam asher avdu baheym b'farech

Maror, these bitter herbs that we eat, what is the meaning of it?

In memory of the bitterness that the Egyptians inflicted on the lives of our ancestors. It is said: and they made their lives bitter with hard labor, with mortar and bricks, work in the fields and every form of slavery that they forced upon them.

בְּכָל דּוֹר וָדוֹר חַיָּב אָדָם לִרְאוֹת אֶת עַצְמוֹ כְּאִלּוּ הוּא יָצָא מִמִּצְרַיִם, שֶׁנֶּאֱמַר: וְהִגַּדְתָּ לְבִנְךָ בַּיּוֹם הַהוּא לֵאמֹר, בַּעֲבוּר זֶה עָשָׂה יְיָ לִי בְּצֵאתִי מִמִּצְרָיִם.

B'chol dor va'dor chayav adam lirot et atsmo ke'ilu hu yatsa m'mitsrayim, she-ne'emar: v'higadta l'vincha bayom hahu l'emor: ba'avur ze asah Adonai li b'tseyti m'mitsrayim.

In every generation, every person must see themselves as though they had been liberated from Egypt, as it is said: and on that day, you shall tell your child all that G-d did for you when He set you free from Egypt.

לֹא אֶת אֲבוֹתֵינוּ בִּלְבָד גָּאַל הַקָּדוֹשׁ בָּרוּךְ הוּא, אֶלָּא אַף אוֹתָנוּ גָּאַל עִמָּהֶם, שֶׁנֶּאֱמַר: וְאוֹתָנוּ הוֹצִיא מִשָּׁם, לְמַעַן הָבִיא אֹתָנוּ, לָתֶת לָנוּ אֶת הָאָרֶץ אֲשֶׁר נִשְׁבַּע לַאֲבֹתֵנוּ.

Lo et avoteynu bilvad ga'al ha-Kadosh Baruch Hu, ela af otanu ga'al imahem, she-ne'emar: v'otanu hotsi mi'sham, l'ma'an hevi otanu, latet lanu et ha-aretz asher nishba l'avoteynu.

Not only our forefathers did G-d, blessed be His name, redeem, but He redeemed us alongside them, as it is said: and He removed us from there, to deliver us, to give us the land that he swore to our ancestors.

לְפִיכָךְ אֲנַחְנוּ חַיָּבִים לְהוֹדוֹת, לְהַלֵּל, לְשַׁבֵּחַ, לְפָאֵר, לְרוֹמֵם, לְהַדֵּר, לְבָרֵךְ, לְעַלֵּה וּלְקַלֵּס לְמִי שֶׁעָשָׂה לַאֲבוֹתֵינוּ וְלָנוּ אֶת כָּל הַנִּסִּים הָאֵלּוּ: הוֹצִיאָנוּ מֵעַבְדוּת לְחֵרוּת מִיָּגוֹן לְשִׂמְחָה, וּמֵאֵבֶל לְיוֹם טוֹב, וּמֵאֲפֵלָה לְאוֹר גָּדוֹל, וּמִשִּׁעְבּוּד לִגְאֻלָּה. וְנֹאמַר לְפָנָיו: הַלְלוּיָהּ.

L'fichach anachnu chayavim l'hodot, l'halel, l'shabeyach, l'fa'er, l'romem, l'hader, l'vareych, l'aleh u'l'kaleys l'mi she-asa l'avoteynu v'lanu et kol ha-nisim ha'eylu: hotsi'anu m'avdut l'cheyrut m'yagon l'simcha, u'm'eyvel l'yom tov, u'm'afeyla l'or gadol, u'm'shi'abud li-g'ula. V'nomar lefanav, halleluyah.

Magid

Therefore, we must give thanks, praise, glorify, exalt, laud, revere, bless, magnify, and extol He who did for our forefathers and for us all of these miracles: delivered us from slavery to freedom, from sorrow to joy, from grief to celebration, from darkness to light, and from subjugation to redemption. And to Him we say, hallelujah.

Halleluya heleylu avdey Adonay haleylu et shem Adonai. Yehi shem Adonai mevorach m'ata v'ad olam. Mi-mizrach shemesh ad mevo'o mehulal shem Adonay. Ram al kol goyim Adonay al ha-shamayim kevodo. Mi k'Adonay eloheynu ha'magbihi lashavet. Ha-mashpili lirot ba-shamayim u'va-aretz. Mekimi m'afar dal m'ashpot yarim evyon. L'hoshivi im nedivim im nedivey amo. Moshivi akeret ha-bayit em ha-banim semeycha halleluyah.

הַלְלוּ יָהּ הַלְלוּ עַבְדֵי יְהוָה הַלְלוּ אֶת שֵׁם יְהוָה. יְהִי שֵׁם יְהוָה מְבֹרָךְ מֵעַתָּה וְעַד עוֹלָם. מִמִּזְרַח שֶׁמֶשׁ עַד מְבוֹאוֹ מְהֻלָּל שֵׁם יְהוָה. רָם עַל כָּל גּוֹיִם יְהוָה עַל הַשָּׁמַיִם כְּבוֹדוֹ. מִי כַּיהוָה אֱלֹהֵינוּ הַמַּגְבִּיהִי לָשָׁבֶת. הַמַּשְׁפִּילִי לִרְאוֹת בַּשָּׁמַיִם וּבָאָרֶץ. מְקִימִי מֵעָפָר דָּל מֵאַשְׁפֹּת יָרִים אֶבְיוֹן. לְהוֹשִׁיבִי עִם נְדִיבִים עִם נְדִיבֵי עַמּוֹ. מוֹשִׁיבִי עֲקֶרֶת הַבַּיִת אֵם הַבָּנִים שְׂמֵחָה הַלְלוּיָהּ.

Praise the Lord, servants of G-d, praise G-d's name. May G-d's name be blessed from now and forever. From the sun in the East until its approach G-d's name is exalted. G-d is greater than any nation and His honor dwells in the sky. Who is like the Lord our G-d, who resides in the heavens. Who deigns to look down upon heavens and earth. He raises the poor from the dust and the needy from the ashes. He puts me with the most generous of His people. He brings joy to the housewife, mother of children. Halleluyah.

בְּצֵאת יִשְׂרָאֵל מִמִּצְרָיִם בֵּית יַעֲקֹב מֵעַם לֹעֵז. הָיְתָה יְהוּדָה לְקָדְשׁוֹ יִשְׂרָאֵל מַמְשְׁלוֹתָיו. הַיָּם רָאָה וַיָּנֹס הַיַּרְדֵּן יִסֹּב לְאָחוֹר. הֶהָרִים רָקְדוּ כְאֵילִים גְּבָעוֹת כִּבְנֵי צֹאן. מַה לְּךָ הַיָּם כִּי תָנוּס הַיַּרְדֵּן תִּסֹּב לְאָחוֹר. הֶהָרִים תִּרְקְדוּ כְאֵילִים גְּבָעוֹת כִּבְנֵי צֹאן. מִלִּפְנֵי אָדוֹן חוּלִי אָרֶץ מִלִּפְנֵי אֱלוֹהַּ יַעֲקֹב. הַהֹפְכִי הַצּוּר אֲגַם מָיִם חַלָּמִישׁ לְמַעְיְנוֹ מָיִם.

B'tseyt Yisrael m'mitzrayim beyt ya'akov me'am lo'ez. Hayta Yehuda l'kodsho Yisrael mamshelotav. Ha-yam ra'ah va-yanos ha-yarden yisov l'achor. He-harim rakdu k'eylim geva'ot kivney tson. Ma lecha ha-yam ki tanus ha-yarden tisov l'achor. He-harim tirkedu k'eylim geva'oy kivney tson. Mi-lifney Adonai chuli aretz mi-lifney eloha ya'akov. Ha-hofchi ha-tsur agam mayim chalamish l-mayno mayim.

When the Israelites left Egypt, when the house of Jacob left that foreign land, thus Jews hold Him sacred and Israel follow Him. The sea beheld and withdrew, the Jordan turned back. The mountains danced like rams, the hills like sheep and goats. Why do you withdraw, sea? Why do you turn back, Jordan? Mountains, dance like rams and hills, dance like sheep and goats. Before the Master of all, before the god of Jacob, the earth bows. You who can turn stone into water, flint into a spring.

Lo ba li לא בא לי

Literally: Hebrew for "It's not coming to me".

Meaning: I don't feel like it.

"I have to go to class but *lo ba li* to listen to my teacher talk for an hour."

Magid

בָּרוּךְ אַתָּה יְיָ אֱלֹהֵינוּ מֶלֶךְ הָעוֹלָם, אֲשֶׁר גְּאָלָנוּ וְגָאַל אֶת אֲבוֹתֵינוּ מִמִּצְרַיִם, וְהִגִּיעָנוּ לַלַּיְלָה הַזֶּה לֶאֱכָל בּוֹ מַצָּה וּמָרוֹר. כֵּן יְיָ אֱלֹהֵינוּ וֵאלֹהֵי אֲבוֹתֵינוּ יַגִּיעֵנוּ לְמוֹעֲדִים וְלִרְגָלִים אֲחֵרִים הַבָּאִים לִקְרָאתֵנוּ לְשָׁלוֹם, שְׂמֵחִים בְּבִנְיַן עִירֶךָ וְשָׂשִׂים בַּעֲבוֹדָתֶךָ. וְנֹאכַל שָׁם מִן הַזְּבָחִים וּמִן הַפְּסָחִים אֲשֶׁר יַגִּיעַ דָּמָם עַל קִיר מִזְבַּחֲךָ לְרָצוֹן, וְנוֹדֶה לְךָ שִׁיר חָדָשׁ עַל גְּאֻלָּתֵנוּ וְעַל פְּדוּת נַפְשֵׁנוּ. בָּרוּךְ אַתָּה יְיָ גָּאַל יִשְׂרָאֵל.

Baruch ata Adonay eloheynu Melech ha-olam, asher ge'alanu v'ga'al et avoteynu mi-mitsrayim, v'hegiyanu la'lalyla hazeh l'echol bo matzah u'maror. Ken Adonay eloheynu v'elohey avoteynu y'gi'eynu l'mo'adim u'l'regalim acherim ha-bai'im likrateynu l'shalom, semeychim b'vinyan irecha v'sasim b'avodatecha. V'nochal sham min ha-zevachim u'min ha-pesachim asher yagiya damam al kir mizbacheycha l'ratzon, v'nodeh lecha shir chadash al ge'ulateynu v'al pedut nafsheynu. Baruch atah Adonay ga'al Yisrael.

Blessed are You, Lord our G-d, King of the universe, who delivered us and our forefathers from Egypt, and brought us to this night, to eat matzah and maror. Lord our G-d, G-d of our ancestors, so You shall deliver us to many forthcoming events and celebrations, and we will be joyful in the resurrection of Your city and happy in doing Your work. And there, we shall eat from the sacrifices and the offerings whose blood shall touch the walls of the altar, and thank you with a new song for our salvation and the redemption of our souls. Blessed are You, G-d, deliverer of Israel.

בָּרוּךְ אַתָּה יְיָ אֱלֹהֵינוּ מֶלֶךְ
הָעוֹלָם בּוֹרֵא פְּרִי הַגָּפֶן.

Baruch atah Adonai Eloheinu melech ha-olam, borei peri ha-gafen.

Blessed are You, Lord our G-d, King of the universe, creator of the fruit of the vine.

 Drink the second cup of wine, reclining to the left.

Magid

Kitsur קיצור

Literally: Hebrew for "short cut".

Meaning: In short, basically.

"I asked him why he was acting so weird. *Kitsur*, turns out he hasn't been feeling well."

Walla וואלה

Literally: Arabic for "by God".

Meaning: huh, really?

"So it turns out next Monday is a holiday, we get the day off."
"*Walla?*"

Israel in Medicine

Given Imaging's PillCam

In 1998, Israeli Gabriel Meron joined Rafael Development Corporation to found Given Imaging, a med-tech company and pioneer of capsule endoscopy technology.

The company has developed, produced, and sold its groundbreaking "PillCam" – a tiny camera ingested through a capsule, which provides live pictures and videos of internal organs in a non-invasive, pain-free way, revolutionizing and modernizing the field of internal medicine.

Rasigiline Parkinson's Drug

Israel's TEVA Pharmaceuticals, one of the largest pharmaceutical companies in the world, is leaps and bounds ahead of its time with its innovative and pioneering medications.

One of its more influential drugs is Rasigiline, used to effectively treat early symptoms of Parkinson's disease. People with Parkinson's struggle with motor skills, with symptoms gradually growing worse as the condition advances. Israeli drug Rasigiline has shown efficacy in both early and advanced Parkinson's and is a truly life-changing solution for a disease once thought to be impossible to manage.

ReWalk

ReWalk is an innovative Israeli invention that has revolutionized the field of assistive technology for individuals with spinal cord injuries. Developed in 2001, ReWalk is a wearable robotic exoskeleton that enables users with paralysis to stand, walk, and even climb stairs independently.

The device works by using motion sensors and motorized joints to mimic natural walking. Users control the exoskeleton through shifts in their weight and movements, allowing them to perform daily activities with greater freedom and mobility.

As the technology continues to advance, ReWalk holds the promise of further enhancing the quality of life for individuals with spinal cord injuries, empowering them to lead more active and fulfilling lives.

Copaxone

Discovered and developed at the prestigious Weitzmann Institute of Science based in Rehovot, Israel, Copaxone is an Israeli-made medication used to treat multiple sclerosis. Included in the World Health Organization's List of Essential Medicines and marketed around the world, this unique drug is a beacon of medical advancement and innovation.

With MS affecting patients' immune systems and leading to deterioration of the nervous system, the availability of a drug that reduces symptoms from the very first episodes is an absolute gamechanger for worldwide health and vitality.

Rachtzah

רַחְצָה

Washing Hands
(this time, with a blessing)

☞ Wash your hands again, pouring water from a cup onto each hand three times.

📜 This time, recite the blessing:

בָּרוּךְ אַתָּה יְיָ אֱלֹהֵינוּ מֶלֶךְ הָעוֹלָם, אֲשֶׁר קִדְּשָׁנוּ בְּמִצְוֹתָיו וְצִוָּנוּ עַל נְטִילַת יָדָיִם.

Baruch atah Adonai Eloheinu melech ha-olam, asher kideshanu b'mitzvotav v'tzivanu al netilat yadayim.

Blessed are You, Lord our G-d, King of the universe, who has sanctified us with His commandments and commanded us to wash our hands.

Al ha-panim על הפנים

Literally: Hebrew for "on the face".

Meaning: terrible, awful.

"How did the job interview go?"
"It was al ha-panim, I totally blew it."

Motzi-Matzah

מוֹצִיא מַצָּה

Blessing on the Matzah

🚩 Pick up the three matzahs – the two whole ones with the broken half in between them – and raise them in the air.

📜 Recite the blessing:

בָּרוּךְ אַתָּה יְיָ אֱלֹהֵינוּ מֶלֶךְ הָעוֹלָם הַמּוֹצִיא לֶחֶם מִן הָאָרֶץ.

Baruch atah Adonai Eloheinu melech ha-olam, ha-motzi lechem min ha-aretz.

Blessed are You, Lord our G-d, King of the universe, who produces bread from the earth.

🚩 Now, remove the bottom matzah from the pile and return it to its place. Holding only the top and middle matzahs, recite the following blessing:

בָּרוּךְ אַתָּה יְיָ אֱלֹהֵינוּ מֶלֶךְ הָעוֹלָם, אֲשֶׁר קִדְּשָׁנוּ בְּמִצְוֹתָיו וְצִוָּנוּ עַל אֲכִילַת מַצָּה.

Baruch atah Adonai Eloheinu melech ha-olam, asher kideshanu b'mitzvotav v'tzivanu al achilat matzah.

Blessed are You, Lord our G-d, King of the universe, who has sanctified us with His commandments and commanded us to eat matzah.

🚩 Break off pieces of the top and middle matzahs and distribute them around the table. The matzah should be eaten while reclining to the left.

Israel in Entertainment

Eurovision Winner Netta Barzilai

Netta Barzilai is widely known for her colorful style and unique sound. Born and raised in a suburb of Tel Aviv, Netta served in the IDF's Navy Band and later studied electronic music at the prestigious Rimon School of Contemporary Music.

Netta found her voice when she was selected to represent Israel at the 2018 Eurovision Contest. Israel had not seen a victory since Dana International's "Diva" in 1998, but Netta dominated the stage and took first place with her instant mega-hit "Toy."

Producer Haim Saban

The Power Rangers and Teenage Mutant Ninja Turtles were a big part of a lot of our childhoods, but did you know both shows were produced by American-Israeli Haim Saban?

Saban grew up in Israel after emigrating from Egypt with his family. He began his entertainment career as a bass player but swiftly moved on to create "Saban Entertainment," and today, his net worth is in the billions.

Saban is a strong supporter of Israel and donates his time and money to many pro-Jewish and pro-Israel causes.

Natalie Portman

Not many people know that famous actress Natalie Portman, known for her roles as Padmé in Star Wars, Nina in Black Swan, and Jane in Thor, was, in fact, born to Israeli parents in Jerusalem and given the name Neta-Lee Hershlag.

Portman's grandparents immigrated to Israel, and Natalie grew up speaking Hebrew and later went on to embody the very spirit of Jewish drive and creativity.

In addition to her significant acting roles, Portman holds a psychology degree from Harvard University. She also studied advanced Hebrew literature and neurobiology.

She is a fierce advocate of animal rights and supports women's rights and anti-poverty causes.

Fauda

Lior Raz and Avi Issacharoff, both former members of the IDF, worked together to create "Fauda" – an Israeli TV series that has gained widespread acclaim for its gripping portrayal of the Israeli-Palestinian conflict.

Through its intense action sequences and multidimensional characters, "Fauda" explores the moral dilemmas faced by Israeli undercover agents, shedding light on the human cost of conflict. The series became internationally successful thanks to its Hollywood-style storytelling and its authenticity in portraying the harsh realities of life in the Middle East.

Maror

מָרוֹר

Bitter Herb

☞ Take a piece of maror (horseradish, lettuce, or another bitter herb) and dip it in the charoset.

📜 Recite the blessing before eating:

בָּרוּךְ אַתָּה יְיָ אֱלֹהֵינוּ מֶלֶךְ הָעוֹלָם, אֲשֶׁר קִדְּשָׁנוּ בְּמִצְוֹתָיו וְצִוָּנוּ עַל אֲכִילַת מָרוֹר.

Baruch atah Adonai Eloheinu melech ha-olam, asher kide-shanu b'mitzvotav v'tzivanu al achilat maror.

Blessed are You, Lord our G-d, King of the universe, who has sanctified us with His commandments and commanded us to eat a bitter herb.

☞ Do not lean while eating the Maror.

Bilti בלתי

Literally: un- prefix.

Meaning: insufferable, impossible.

"This guy at the store was taking ages to pay, he was *bilti*."

Korech

כּוֹרֵךְ

Maror Wrapped in Matzah

☞ Take two pieces of matzah, put some maror between them, and dip everything in the charoset. You may also spread the charoset on the matzah, add the maror and eat it like a sandwich.

📜 Recite before eating:

זֵכֶר לְמִקְדָּשׁ כְּהִלֵּל. כֵּן עָשָׂה הִלֵּל בִּזְמַן שֶׁבֵּית הַמִּקְדָּשׁ הָיָה קַיָּם: הָיָה כּוֹרֵךְ פֶּסַח מַצָּה וּמָרוֹר וְאוֹכֵל בְּיַחַד, לְקַיֵּם מַה שֶּׁנֶּאֱמַר: עַל מַצּוֹת וּמְרֹרִים יֹאכְלֻהוּ.

Zecher l'mikdash k'hillel. Ken asah hillel bizman she-beyt ha-mikdash hayah kayam. Hayah korech pesach matzah umaror v'ochel beyachad, lekayem mah she-ne'emar: al matzot umerowrim yocheluhu.

In memory of the custom of Hillel in the days of the Temple. So Hillel would do while there was a temple: he would wrap the matzah with the maror and eat them together, to observe what is commanded: You shall eat it (the Passover sacrifice) on matzah and maror.

☞ Recline to the left and eat the maror sandwich.

Shulchan-Orech

שֻׁלְחָן עוֹרֵךְ

The Festive Meal

☞ Now is the time to sit back, relax, and enjoy a delicious festive meal.

☞ At this point, it is customary to eat the hard-boiled egg from the Seder plate, dipped in salt water.

סבבה *Sababa*

Literally: Arabic for "fierce yearning".

Meaning: ok, cool.

"Oh, you signed up for the lecture? *Sababa*, I'll join you."

Israel in Entrepreneurship

Chef Eyal Shani

Chef Eyal Shani has made waves in the culinary world with his bold and innovative approach to food. Hailing from Israel, Shani is renowned for his unconventional cooking techniques and his love for simplicity and quality ingredients.

His international entrepreneurial success stems from his ability to create unique dining experiences that resonate with food lovers worldwide. Shani has expanded his culinary empire beyond Israel, with restaurants in various cities around the globe, including Paris, New York, and Melbourne.

With a Michelin Star for his NYC restaurant, Shmoné, Shani's food is enjoyed and appreciated by Israelis, Jews, and Gentiles alike everywhere in the world.

Moovit App

Moovit, an Israeli transportation app founded in 2012, has revolutionized the way people navigate urban transit systems worldwide.

What sets Moovit apart is its crowd-sourced data, which gathers information from users to offer accurate and up-to-date transit information. This crowdsourcing model, similar to Israeli navigation app Waze, enables Moovit to provide comprehensive coverage in cities across the globe, making it a valuable tool for travelers and locals alike.

Israelis may not be known for their courteous road manners, but you can be sure that in innovation and technology Israel keeps far ahead of its time!

Check Point

With a focus on proactive threat prevention and detection, renowned Israeli cybersecurity company Check Point Software Technologies has earned a reputation for its advanced technologies that defend against cyber threats, including malware, ransomware, and phishing attacks.

Israel is no stranger to cybersecurity threats and as a result has a flourishing cybersecurity community, with many of its leaders training and graduating from its prestigious military agencies. Check Point protects not only Israeli networks, but has solidified its position as a key player in the cybersecurity industry, helping safeguard data and devices for millions of users worldwide.

Playtech

Playtech is an Israeli-founded, globally renowned technology company specializing in the development and provision of online gaming software and services. The company's portfolio includes casino games, live dealer games, sports betting platforms, and virtual sports, among other offerings.

With a vast global presence spanning Europe, Asia, and the Americas, Playtech serves as a trusted partner to some of the world's largest and most reputable gambling operators. Its cutting-edge technology, extensive game portfolio, and commitment to excellence have helped them bring enjoyment and excitement to millions.

Tzafun

צָפוּן

The Afikoman

☞ Now that you've finished the meal, it's time to reveal the Afikoman.

☞ If you hid it earlier in the evening, now is the time for whoever found it during the Seder to reveal it.

☞ The Afikoman is the last thing we eat during the Seder night. Break off pieces of the Afikoman matzah and distribute them around the table. Eat the matzah while reclining to your left.

Barech

בָּרֵךְ

Blessing After the Meal

Pour the third cup of wine.

 Recite the blessing on the wine:

בָּרוּךְ אַתָּה יְיָ אֱלֹהֵינוּ מֶלֶךְ הָעוֹלָם בּוֹרֵא פְּרִי הַגָּפֶן.

Baruch atah Adonai Eloheinu melech ha-olam, borei peri ha-gafen.

Blessed are You, Lord our G-d, King of the universe, creator of the fruit of the vine.

 Drink the third cup of wine, while reclining to the left.

 Pour the fourth cup of wine.

 It is customary to pour an extra cup of wine for Elijah the Prophet, who is said to visit on Seder night. Open the front door to invite him in.

Recite the following:

שְׁפֹךְ חֲמָתְךָ אֶל הַגּוֹיִם אֲשֶׁר לֹא יְדָעוּךָ וְעַל מַמְלָכוֹת אֲשֶׁר בְּשִׁמְךָ לֹא קָרָאוּ. כִּי אָכַל אֶת יַעֲקֹב וְאֶת נָוֵהוּ הֵשַׁמּוּ. שְׁפֹךְ עֲלֵיהֶם זַעְמֶךָ וַחֲרוֹן אַפְּךָ יַשִּׂיגֵם. תִּרְדֹּף בְּאַף וְתַשְׁמִידֵם מִתַּחַת שְׁמֵי יְיָ.

Shefoch chamatcha el ha-goy-im asher lo yeda'ucha v'al mam-lachot asher b'shimcha lo kar'u. Ki achal et ya'akov v'et navehu heyshamu. Shefoch aleyhem za'amcha v'charon apcha yasi-gem. Tirdof b'af v'tashmidem mitachat shmey Adonai.

Unleash Your wrath upon the nations who do not acknowledge You and upon the kingdoms who do not call Your Name. For they have devoured Jacob and destroyed his land. Unleash Your fury upon them and let Your anger seize them. Pursue them with rage and destroy them beneath G-d's heavens.

Some sing Eliyahu Ha'navi, which can be found in the "Songs" section on page 96.

You may now close the front door.

באסה *Basa*

Literally: Arabic for "miserable".

Meaning: bummer, that sucks.

"I waited for my blind date but she never showed. It was a real *basa*."

בול *Bool*

Literally: from English, "Bull's Eye".

Meaning: exactly, jackpot.

"I chose *bool* the right color bag for this outfit!"

Hallel

הַלֵּל

Praise to G-d

הִנְנִי מוּכָן וּמְזֻמָּן לְקַיֵּם מִצְוַת כּוֹס רְבִיעִי שֶׁהוּא כְּנֶגֶד בְּשׂוֹרַת הַיְשׁוּעָה, שֶׁאָמַר הַקָּדוֹשׁ בָּרוּךְ הוּא לְיִשְׂרָאֵל "וְלָקַחְתִּי אֶתְכֶם לִי לְעָם וְהָיִיתִי לָכֶם לֵאלֹהִים."

Hineyni muchan u'mezuman l'kayem mitzvat kos revi'i she-hu k'negged besorat ha-yeshu'a, she-amar ha-Kadosh Baruch Hu l'Yisrael, "v'lakachti etchem li l'am v'hayiti lachem l'elohim."

I am ready and willing to observe the commandment of the fourth cup, which signifies the tidings of salvation, as G-d said to the people of Israel: "and I will take you in as my people and I shall be your god."

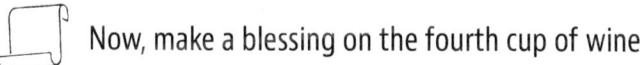 Now, make a blessing on the fourth cup of wine:

בָּרוּךְ אַתָּה יְיָ אֱלֹהֵינוּ מֶלֶךְ הָעוֹלָם בּוֹרֵא פְּרִי הַגָּפֶן.

Baruch atah Adonai Eloheinu melech ha-olam, borei peri ha-gafen.

Blessed are You, Lord our G-d, King of the universe, creator of the fruit of the vine.

 Drink the fourth and final cup of wine while reclining to the left.

 Recite the final blessing after drinking wine:

בָּרוּךְ אַתָּה יְיָ אֱלֹהֵינוּ מֶלֶךְ הָעוֹלָם, עַל הַגֶּפֶן וְעַל פְּרִי הַגֶּפֶן, עַל תְּנוּבַת הַשָּׂדֶה וְעַל אֶרֶץ חֶמְדָּה טוֹבָה וּרְחָבָה שֶׁרָצִיתָ וְהִנְחַלְתָּ לַאֲבוֹתֵינוּ לֶאֱכֹל מִפִּרְיָהּ וְלִשְׂבֹּעַ מִטּוּבָהּ.

Baruch atah Adonai Eloheinu melech ha-olam, al ha-gefen v'al peri ha-gefen, al tnuvat ha-sadeh v'al eretz chemda tova u'rechava she-ratsita v'hinchalta l'avoteynu le'echol m'pirya v'lisbo'a mituva.

Blessed are You, Lord our G-d, King of the universe, for the vines and the fruit of the vines, for the produce of the field, and for the good, beautiful and vast country which You chose to give to our ancestors so that we may eat from its fruit and be satiated by its goodness.

רַחֵם נָא יְיָ אֱלֹהֵינוּ עַל יִשְׂרָאֵל עַמֶּךָ וְעַל יְרוּשָׁלַיִם עִירֶךָ וְעַל צִיּוֹן מִשְׁכַּן כְּבוֹדֶךָ וְעַל מִזְבְּחֶךָ וְעַל הֵיכָלֶךָ וּבְנֵה יְרוּשָׁלַיִם עִיר הַקֹּדֶשׁ בִּמְהֵרָה בְיָמֵינוּ וְהַעֲלֵנוּ לְתוֹכָהּ וְשַׂמְּחֵנוּ בְּבִנְיָנָהּ וְנֹאכַל מִפִּרְיָהּ וְנִשְׂבַּע מִטּוּבָהּ וּנְבָרֶכְךָ עָלֶיהָ בִּקְדֻשָּׁה וּבְטָהֳרָה.

Rachem na Adonai Eloheinu al Yisrael amcha v'al yerushalayim irecha v'al tsion mishkan kevodecha v'al mizbachecha v'al heichalecha u'vney yerushalayim ir ha-kodesh bimhera b'yameynu v'ha'aleynu l'tochah v'samchenu b'vinyanah v'nochal m'pirya v'nisba mituva u'nevarechecha aleyha b'kdusha uv'tahara.

Please have mercy, Lord our G-d, on Israel Your people, on Jerusalem Your city, on Zion, Your place of rest, on Your altar and Your hall. Rebuild the holy city of Jerusalem in our time and let us ascend to it and be joyous in its grandeur. Then we shall eat from its fruit and be satiated by its goodness and bless You for it with sanctity and purity.

בְּשַׁבָּת: וּרְצֵה וְהַחֲלִיצֵנוּ בְּיוֹם הַשַּׁבָּת הַזֶּה) וְשַׂמְּחֵנוּ בְּיוֹם חַג הַמַּצּוֹת הַזֶּה, כִּי אַתָּה יְיָ טוֹב וּמֵטִיב לַכֹּל וְנוֹדֶה לְּךָ עַל הָאָרֶץ וְעַל פְּרִי הַגָּפֶן.

(on Shabbat: u'retsey v'hachalitseynu b'yom ha-shabbat hazeh) v'samcheynu b'yom chag ha-matzot hazeh, ki atah Adonai tov u'meytiv lakol v'nodeh lecha al ha'aretz v'al peri ha-gafen.

(On Shabbat: Give us strength on this Sabbath day and) let us be happy on this festival of Matzah, because You are good and benevolent to all and we will thank You for the land and for the fruit of the vine.

בָּרוּךְ אַתָּה יְיָ עַל הָאָרֶץ וְעַל פְּרִי הַגָּפֶן.

Baruch ata Adonai, al ha'aretz v'al peri ha-gafen.

Blessed are You, G-d, for the land and for the fruit of the vine.

Israel in Sports

Krav Maga

Developed by the IDF, Krav Maga (literally: contact combat) is a form of self-defense martial arts designed to focus on hand-to-hand urban fighting. It is a complex martial art that has been developed over time and adopted by Israel's military, police, and even civilians. It is taught around the world as a measure of self-defense, keeping people everywhere safe in their daily lives, thanks to Israeli military innovation.

Keep an eye out for Krav Maga in popular culture – it has been studied by some of Hollywood's leading action actors like Tom Cruise, Daniel Craig, and even J-Lo!

Olympic Gold Medalist Linoy Ashram

The 2022 Tokyo Olympics saw an unprecedented series of successes for Israeli sports. Among these and perhaps most notably was gold-medalist Linoy Ashram, who defied all odds and beat out intimidating competition to win the individual all-around rhythmic gymnastics competition.

Linoy's graceful and skillful performance left no doubt as to her expertise and how deserving she was of the title and medal. Beyond her many athletic accomplishments, Linoy serves as an inspiration to aspiring gymnasts worldwide. Her success has helped elevate the profile of rhythmic gymnastics and has brought Israeli gymnastics to the forefront.

NBA Stars Omri Casspi & Deni Avdija

For a long time, the prestigious NBA league seemed far from Israeli athletes' reach. That was, until Holon-born Omri Casspi made history by becoming the first Israeli to be drafted into the NBA when he was selected by the Sacramento Kings in the first round of the 2009 NBA Draft.

Casspi's success led many young Israeli athletes to set their sights on greater things, and in 2020, fellow Israeli Deni Avdija again took the world by storm when he was picked by the Washington Wizards.

Both Casspi and Avdija embody the spirit of hard work, talent, and perseverance, and both are vocal in their support of young athletes, particularly those hailing from their own homeland.

Tennis Champion Shahar Pe'er

Shahar Pe'er is a former professional tennis player from Israel who achieved considerable success during her career. Pe'er began playing tennis at a young age and quickly rose through the ranks, establishing herself as one of Israel's most promising tennis talents.

Her greatest professional achievement was ranking a career-high singles ranking of World No. 11 and doubles ranking of World No. 14. She competed in numerous Grand Slam tournaments, including the Australian Open, French Open, Wimbledon, and US Open, consistently showcasing her skill on the court.

Off the court, Pe'er served as a proud ambassador for Israeli tennis, inspiring young athletes and promoting the sport in her home country. Her achievements and contributions to Israeli tennis have left a lasting legacy, cementing her status as one of Israel's most accomplished athletes.

Nirtzah

נִרְצָה

Conclusion of the Seder

At the conclusion of the Seder, we celebrate having been able to come together for the festivities and look forward to a prosperous and happy year. Everyone sings together:

לְשָׁנָה הַבָּאָה בִּירוּשָׁלָיִם.   L'shana haba'ah b'Yerushalayim

Next year in Jerusalem!

Songs

Chad Gadya – One Little Goat

חַד גַּדְיָא, חַד גַּדְיָא, דְּזַבִּין אַבָּא בִּתְרֵי זוּזֵי, חַד גַּדְיָא,חַד גַּדְיָא.

וְאָתָא שׁוּנְרָא וְאָכְלָה לְגַדְיָא, דְּזַבִּין אַבָּא בִּתְרֵי זוּזֵי, חַד גַּדְיָא.

וְאָתָא כַלְבָּא וְנָשַׁךְ לְשׁוּנְרָא, דְּאָכְלָה לְגַדְיָא, דְּזַבִּין אַבָּא בִּתְרֵי זוּזֵי, חַד גַּדְיָא,חַד גַּדְיָא.

וְאָתָא חוּטְרָא וְהִכָּה לְכַלְבָּא, דְּנָשַׁךְ לְשׁוּנְרָא, דְּאָכְלָה לְגַדְיָא, דְּזַבִּין אַבָּא בִּתְרֵי זוּזֵי, חַד גַּדְיָא,חַד גַּדְיָא.

וְאָתָא נוּרָא וְשָׂרַף לְחוּטְרָא, דְּהִכָּה לְכַלְבָּא, דְּנָשַׁךְ לְשׁוּנְרָא, דְּאָכְלָה לְגַדְיָא, דְּזַבִּין אַבָּא בִּתְרֵי זוּזֵי, חַד גַּדְיָא, חַד גַּדְיָא.

וְאָתָא מַיָּא וְכָבָה לְנוּרָא, דְּשָׂרַף לְחוּטְרָא, דְּהִכָּה לְכַלְבָּא, דְּנָשַׁךְ לְשׁוּנְרָא, דְּאָכְלָה לְגַדְיָא, דְּזַבִּין אַבָּא בִּתְרֵי זוּזֵי, חַד גַּדְיָא,חַד גַּדְיָא.

וְאָתָא תוֹרָא וְשָׁתָה לְמַיָּא, דְּכָבָה לְנוּרָא, דְּשָׂרַף לְחוּטְרָא, דְּהִכָּה לְכַלְבָּא, דְּנָשַׁךְ לְשׁוּנְרָא, דְּאָכְלָה לְגַדְיָא, דְּזַבִּין אַבָּא בִּתְרֵי זוּזֵי, חַד גַּדְיָא,חַד גַּדְיָא.

Chad gadya, chad gadya, d'zabin aba b'trei zuzei, chad gadya, chad gadya.

V'ata shunra v'achla l'gadya, d'zabin aba b'trei zuzei, chad gadya, chad gadya.

V'ata chalba v'nashach l'shunra, d'achla l'gadya, d'zabin aba b'trei zuzei, chad gadya, chad gadya.

V'ata chutra v'hica l'calba, d'nashach l'shunra, d'achla l'gadya, d'zabin aba b'trei zuzei, chad gadya, chad gadya.

V'ata nura v'saraf l'chutra, d'hica l'calba, d'nashach l'shunra, d'achla l'gadya, d'zabin aba b'trei zuzei, chad gadya, chad gadya.

V'ata maya v'chaba l'nura, d'saraf l'chutra, d'hica l'calba, d'nashach l'shunra, d'achla l'gadya, d'zabin aba b'trei zuzei, chad gadya, chad gadya.

V'ata tora v'shata l'maya, d'chaba l'nura, d'saraf l'chutra, d'hica l'calba, d'nashach l'shunra, d'achla l'gadya, d'zabin aba b'trei zuzei, chad gadya, chad gadya.

וְאָתָא הַשׁוֹחֵט וְשָׁחַט לְתוֹרָא, דְּשָׁתָה לְמַיָּא, דְּכָבָה לְנוּרָא, דְּשָׂרַף לְחוּטְרָא, דְּהִכָּה לְכַלְבָּא, דְּנָשַׁךְ לְשׁוּנְרָא, דְּאָכְלָה לְגַדְיָא, דְּזַבִּין אַבָּא בִּתְרֵי זוּזֵי, חַד גַּדְיָא, חַד גַּדְיָא.

V'ata hashochet v'shachat l'tora, d'shata l'maya, d'chaba l'nura, d'saraf l'chutra, d'hica l'calba, d'nashach l'shunra, d'achla l'gadya, d'zabin aba b'trei zuzei, chad gadya, chad gadya.

וְאָתָא מַלְאַךְ הַמָּוֶת וְשָׁחַט לְשׁוֹחֵט, דְּשָׁחַט לְתוֹרָא, דְּשָׁתָה לְמַיָּא, דְּכָבָה לְנוּרָא, דְּשָׂרַף לְחוּטְרָא, דְּהִכָּה לְכַלְבָּא, דְּנָשַׁךְ לְשׁוּנְרָא, דְּאָכְלָה לְגַדְיָא, דְּזַבִּין אַבָּא בִּתְרֵי זוּזֵי, חַד גַּדְיָא, חַד גַּדְיָא.

V'ata malach hamavet v'shachat l'shochet, d'shachat l'tora, d'shata l'maya, d'chaba l'nura, d'saraf l'chutra, d'hica l'calba, d'nashach l'shunra, d'achla l'gadya, d'zabin aba b'trei zuzei, chad gadya, chad gadya.

וְאָתָא הַקָּדוֹשׁ בָּרוּךְ הוּא וְשָׁחַט לְמַלְאַךְ הַמָּוֶת, דְּשָׁחַט לְשׁוֹחֵט, דְּשָׁחַט לְתוֹרָא, דְּשָׁתָה לְמַיָּא, דְּכָבָה לְנוּרָא, דְּשָׂרַף לְחוּטְרָא, דְּהִכָּה לְכַלְבָּא, דְּנָשַׁךְ לְשׁוּנְרָא, דְּאָכְלָה לְגַדְיָא דְּזַבִּין אַבָּא בִּתְרֵי זוּזֵי, חַד גַּדְיָא, חַד גַּדְיָא.

V'ata ha-Kadosh Baruch Hu, v'ishachat l'malach hamavet, d'shachat l'shochet, d'shachat l'tora, d'shata l'maya, d'chaba l'nura, d'saraf l'chutra, d'hica l'calba, d'nashach l'shunra, d'achla l'gadya, d'zabin aba b'trei zuzei, chad gadya, chad gadya.

One little goat, one little goat that father bought for two zuzim. One little goat, one little goat.

Along came a cat and ate the goat that father bought for two zuzim. One little goat, one little goat.

Along came a dog and bit the cat that ate the goat that father bought for two zuzim. One little goat, one little goat.

Along came a stick and hit the dog that bit the cat that ate the goat that father bought for two zuzim. One little goat, one little goat.

Along came a fire and burned the stick that hit the dog that bit the cat that ate the goat that father bought for two zuzim. One little goat, one little goat.

Along came some water and put out the fire that burned the stick that hit the dog that bit the cat that ate the goat that father bought for two zuzim. One little goat, one little goat.

Along came an ox and drank the water that put out the fire that burned the stick that hit the dog that bit the cat that ate the goat that father bought for two zuzim. One little goat, one little goat.

Along came a butcher and slaughtered the ox that drank the water that put out the fire that burned the stick that hit the dog that bit the cat that ate the goat that father bought for two zuzim. One little goat, one little goat.

Along came the angel of death and slaughtered the butcher who slaughtered the ox that drank the water that put out the fire that burned the stick that hit the dog that bit the cat that ate the goat that father bought for two zuzim. One little goat, one little goat.

Then along came the Holy One, Blessed be He, and slaughtered the angel of death who slaughtered the butcher who slaughtered the ox that drank the water that put out the fire that burned the stick that hit the dog that bit the cat that ate the goat that father bought for two zuzim. One little goat, one little goat.

Echad Mi Yodeya – Who Knows One?

אֶחָד מִי יוֹדֵעַ? אֶחָד אֲנִי יוֹדֵעַ. אֶחָד אֱלֹהֵינוּ שֶׁבַּשָּׁמַיִם וּבָאָרֶץ.

Echad mi yodea? Echad ani yodea. Echad Eloheinu she-bashamayim u'va'aretz.

שְׁנַיִם מִי יוֹדֵעַ? שְׁנַיִם אֲנִי יוֹדֵעַ. שְׁנֵי לוּחוֹת הַבְּרִית, אֶחָד אֱלֹהֵינוּ שֶׁבַּשָּׁמַיִם וּבָאָרֶץ.

Shnayim mi yodea? Shnayim ani yodea. Shnei luchot ha-brit, echad Eloheinu she-bashamayim u'va'aretz.

שְׁלֹשָׁה מִי יוֹדֵעַ? שְׁלֹשָׁה אֲנִי יוֹדֵעַ. שְׁלֹשָׁה אָבוֹת, שְׁנֵי לוּחוֹת הַבְּרִית, אֶחָד אֱלֹהֵינוּ שֶׁבַּשָּׁמַיִם וּבָאָרֶץ.

Shloshah mi yodea? Shloshah ani yodea. Shloshah avot, shnei luchot ha-brit, echad Eloheinu she-bashamayim u'va'aretz.

אַרְבַּע מִי יוֹדֵעַ? אַרְבַּע אֲנִי יוֹדֵעַ. אַרְבַּע אִמָּהוֹת, שְׁלֹשָׁה אָבוֹת, שְׁנֵי לוּחוֹת הַבְּרִית, אֶחָד אֱלֹהֵינוּ שֶׁבַּשָּׁמַיִם וּבָאָרֶץ.

Arbah mi yodea? Arbah ani yodea. Arbah imahot, shloshah avot, shnei luchot ha-brit, echad Eloheinu she-bashamayim u'va'aretz.

חֲמִשָּׁה מִי יוֹדֵעַ? חֲמִשָּׁה אֲנִי יוֹדֵעַ. חֲמִשָּׁה חֻמְשֵׁי תוֹרָה, אַרְבַּע אִמָּהוֹת, שְׁלֹשָׁה אָבוֹת, שְׁנֵי לוּחוֹת הַבְּרִית, אֶחָד אֱלֹהֵינוּ שֶׁבַּשָּׁמַיִם וּבָאָרֶץ.

Chamishah mi yodea? Chamishah ani yodea. Chamishah chumshei Torah, arbah imahot, shloshah avot, shnei luchot ha-brit, echad Eloheinu she-bashamayim u'va'aretz.

שִׁשָּׁה מִי יוֹדֵעַ? שִׁשָּׁה אֲנִי יוֹדֵעַ. שִׁשָּׁה סִדְרֵי מִשְׁנָה, חֲמִשָּׁה חֻמְשֵׁי תוֹרָה, אַרְבַּע אִמָּהוֹת, שְׁלֹשָׁה אָבוֹת שְׁנֵי לוּחוֹת הַבְּרִית, אֶחָד אֱלֹהֵינוּ שֶׁבַּשָּׁמַיִם וּבָאָרֶץ.

Shishah mi yodea? Shishah ani yodea. Shishah sidrei mishnah, chamishah chumshei Torah, arbah imahot, shloshah avot, shnei luchot ha-brit, echad Eloheinu she-bashamayim u'va'aretz.

שִׁבְעָה מִי יוֹדֵעַ? שִׁבְעָה אֲנִי יוֹדֵעַ. שִׁבְעָה יְמֵי שַׁבַּתָּא, שִׁשָּׁה סִדְרֵי מִשְׁנָה, חֲמִשָּׁה חֻמְשֵׁי תוֹרָה, אַרְבַּע אִמָּהוֹת, שְׁלֹשָׁה אָבוֹת, שְׁנֵי לוּחוֹת הַבְּרִית, אֶחָד אֱלֹהֵינוּ שֶׁבַּשָּׁמַיִם וּבָאָרֶץ.

שְׁמוֹנָה מִי יוֹדֵעַ? שְׁמוֹנָה אֲנִי יוֹדֵעַ. שְׁמוֹנָה יְמֵי מִילָה, שִׁבְעָה יְמֵי שַׁבַּתָּא, שִׁשָּׁה סִדְרֵי מִשְׁנָה, חֲמִשָּׁה חֻמְשֵׁי תוֹרָה, אַרְבַּע אִמָּהוֹת, שְׁלֹשָׁה אָבוֹת, שְׁנֵי לוּחוֹת הַבְּרִית, אֶחָד אֱלֹהֵינוּ שֶׁבַּשָּׁמַיִם וּבָאָרֶץ.

תִּשְׁעָה מִי יוֹדֵעַ? תִּשְׁעָה אֲנִי יוֹדֵעַ. תִּשְׁעָה יַרְחֵי לֵדָה, שְׁמוֹנָה יְמֵי מִילָה, שִׁבְעָה יְמֵי שַׁבַּתָּא, שִׁשָּׁה סִדְרֵי מִשְׁנָה, חֲמִשָּׁה חֻמְשֵׁי תוֹרָה, אַרְבַּע אִמָּהוֹת, שְׁלֹשָׁה אָבוֹת, שְׁנֵי לוּחוֹת הַבְּרִית, אֶחָד אֱלֹהֵינוּ שֶׁבַּשָּׁמַיִם וּבָאָרֶץ.

עֲשָׂרָה מִי יוֹדֵעַ? עֲשָׂרָה אֲנִי יוֹדֵעַ. עֲשָׂרָה דִבְּרַיָּא, תִּשְׁעָה יַרְחֵי לֵדָה, שְׁמוֹנָה יְמֵי מִילָה, שִׁבְעָה יְמֵי שַׁבַּתָּא, שִׁשָּׁה סִדְרֵי מִשְׁנָה, חֲמִשָּׁה חֻמְשֵׁי תוֹרָה, אַרְבַּע אִמָּהוֹת, שְׁלֹשָׁה אָבוֹת, שְׁנֵי לוּחוֹת הַבְּרִית, אֶחָד אֱלֹהֵינוּ שֶׁבַּשָּׁמַיִם וּבָאָרֶץ.

Shivah mi yodea? Shivah ani yodea. Shivah y'mei shabtah, shishah sidrei mishnah, chamishah chumshei Torah, arbah imahot, shloshah avot, shnei luchot ha-brit, echad Eloheinu she-bashamayim u'va'aretz.

Shmonah mi yodea? Shmonah ani yodea. Shmonah y'mei milah, shivah y'mei shabtah, shishah sidrei mishnah, chamishah chumshei Torah, arbah imahot, shloshah avot, shnei luchot ha-brit, echad Eloheinu she-bashamayim u'va'aretz.

Tishah mi yodea? Tishah ani yodea. Tishah yarchei leidah, shmonah y'mei milah, shivah y'mei shabtah, shishah sidrei mishnah, chamishah chumshei Torah, arbah imahot, shloshah avot, shnei luchot ha-brit, echad Eloheinu she-bashamayim u'va'aretz.

Asarah mi yodea? Asarah ani yodea. Asarah dibrayah, tishah yarchei leidah, shmonah y'mei milah, shivah y'mei shabtah, shishah sidrei mishnah, chamishah chumshei Torah, arbah imahot, shloshah avot, shnei luchot ha-brit, echad Eloheinu she-bashamayim u'va'aretz.

Songs

אַחַד עָשָׂר מִי יוֹדֵעַ? אַחַד עָשָׂר אֲנִי יוֹדֵעַ. אַחַד עָשָׂר כּוֹכְבַיָּא, עֲשָׂרָה דִבְּרַיָּא, תִּשְׁעָה יַרְחֵי לֵדָה, שְׁמוֹנָה יְמֵי מִילָה, שִׁבְעָה יְמֵי שַׁבְּתָא, שִׁשָּׁה סִדְרֵי מִשְׁנָה, חֲמִשָּׁה חֻמְשֵׁי תוֹרָה, אַרְבַּע אִמָּהוֹת, שְׁלֹשָׁה אָבוֹת, שְׁנֵי לוּחוֹת הַבְּרִית, אֶחָד אֱלֹהֵינוּ שֶׁבַּשָּׁמַיִם וּבָאָרֶץ.

Achad-asar mi yodea? Achad-asar ani yodea. Achad-asar kochvayah, asarah dibrayah, tishah yarchei leidah, shmonah y'mei milah, shivah y'mei shabtah, shishah sidrei mishnah, chamishah chumshei Torah, arbah imahot, shloshah avot, shnei luchot ha-brit, echad Eloheinu she-bashamayim u'va'aretz.

שְׁנֵים עָשָׂר מִי יוֹדֵעַ? שְׁנֵים עָשָׂר אֲנִי יוֹדֵעַ. שְׁנֵים עָשָׂר שִׁבְטַיָּא, אַחַד עָשָׂר כּוֹכְבַיָּא, עֲשָׂרָה דִבְּרַיָּא, תִּשְׁעָה יַרְחֵי לֵדָה, שְׁמוֹנָה יְמֵי מִילָה, שִׁבְעָה יְמֵי שַׁבְּתָא, שִׁשָּׁה סִדְרֵי מִשְׁנָה, חֲמִשָּׁה חֻמְשֵׁי תוֹרָה, אַרְבַּע אִמָּהוֹת, שְׁלֹשָׁה אָבוֹת, שְׁנֵי לוּחוֹת הַבְּרִית, אֶחָד אֱלֹהֵינוּ שֶׁבַּשָּׁמַיִם וּבָאָרֶץ.

Shneim-asar mi yodea? Shneim-asar ani yodea. Shneim-asar shivtayah, achad-asar kochvayah, asarah dibrayah, tishah yarchei leidah, shmonah y'mei milah, shivah y'mei shabtah, shishah sidrei mishnah, chamishah chumshei Torah, arbah imahot, shloshah avot, shnei luchot ha-brit, echad Eloheinu she-bashamayim u'va'aretz.

שְׁלֹשָׁה עָשָׂר מִי יוֹדֵעַ? שְׁלֹשָׁה עָשָׂר אֲנִי יוֹדֵעַ. שְׁלֹשָׁה עָשָׂר מִדַּיָּא, שְׁנֵים עָשָׂר שִׁבְטַיָּא, אַחַד עָשָׂר כּוֹכְבַיָּא, עֲשָׂרָה דִבְּרַיָּא, תִּשְׁעָה יַרְחֵי לֵדָה, שְׁמוֹנָה יְמֵי מִילָה, שִׁבְעָה יְמֵי שַׁבְּתָא, שִׁשָּׁה סִדְרֵי מִשְׁנָה, חֲמִשָּׁה חֻמְשֵׁי תוֹרָה, אַרְבַּע אִמָּהוֹת, שְׁלֹשָׁה אָבוֹת, שְׁנֵי לוּחוֹת הַבְּרִית, אֶחָד אֱלֹהֵינוּ שֶׁבַּשָּׁמַיִם וּבָאָרֶץ.

Shloshah-asar mi yodea? Shloshah-asar ani yodea. Shloshah-asar midayah, shneim-asar shivtayah, achad-asar kochvayah, asarah dibrayah, tishah yarchei leidah, shmonah y'mei milah, shivah y'mei shabtah, shishah sidrei mishnah, chamishah chumshei Torah, arbah imahot, shloshah avot, shnei luchot ha-brit, echad Eloheinu she-bashamayim u'va'aretz.

Who knows one? I know one. One is our G-d in Heaven and Earth.

Who knows two? I know two. Two are the tablets of the covenant. One is our G-d in Heaven and Earth.

Who knows three? I know three. Three are the patriarchs. Two are the tablets of the covenant. One is our G-d in Heaven and Earth.

Who knows four? I know four. Four are the matriarchs. Three are the patriarchs. Two are the tablets of the covenant. One is our G-d in Heaven and Earth.

Who knows five? I know five. Five are the books of the Torah. Four are the matriarchs. Three are the patriarchs. Two are the tablets of the covenant. One is our G-d in Heaven and Earth.

Who knows six? I know six. Six are the orders of the Mishnah. Five are the books of the Torah. Four are the matriarchs. Three are the patriarchs. Two are the tablets of the covenant. One is our G-d in Heaven and Earth.

Who knows seven? I know seven. Seven are the days of the week. Six are the orders of the Mishnah. Five are the books of the Torah. Four are the matriarchs. Three are the patriarchs. Two are the tablets of the covenant. One is our G-d in Heaven and Earth

Who knows eight? I know eight. Eight are the days for circumcision. Seven are the days of the week. Six are the orders of the Mishnah. Five are the books of the Torah. Four are the matriarchs. Three are the patriarchs. Two are the tablets of the covenant. One is our G-d in Heaven and Earth.

Who knows nine? I know nine. Nine are the months of childbirth. Eight are the days for circumcision. Seven are the days of the week. Six are the orders of the Mishnah. Five are the books of the Torah. Four are the matriarchs. Three are the patriarchs. Two are the tablets of the covenant. One is our G-d in Heaven and Earth.

Who knows ten? I know ten. Ten are the Words from Sinai. Nine are the months of childbirth. Eight are the days for circumcision. Seven are the days of the week. Six are the orders of the Mishnah. Five are the books of the Torah. Four are the matriarchs. Three are the patriarchs. Two are the tablets of the covenant. One is our G-d in Heaven and Earth.

Who knows eleven? I know eleven. Eleven are the stars. Ten are the Words from Sinai. Nine are the months of childbirth. Eight are the days for circumcision. Seven are the days of the week. Six are the orders of the Mishnah. Five are the books of the Torah. Four are the matriarchs. Three are the patriarchs. Two are the tablets of the covenant. One is our G-d in Heaven and Earth.

Who knows twelve? I know twelve. Twelve are the tribes. Eleven are the stars. Ten are the Words from Sinai. Nine are the months of childbirth. Eight are the days for circumcision. Seven are the days of the week. Six are the orders of the Mishnah. Five are the books of the Torah. Four are the matriarchs. Three are the patriarchs. Two are the tablets of the covenant. One is our G-d in Heaven and Earth.

Who knows thirteen? I know thirteen. Thirteen are the attributes of G-d. Twelve are the tribes. Eleven are the stars. Ten are the Words from Sinai. Nine are the months of childbirth. Eight are the days for circumcision. Seven are the days of the week. Six are the orders of the Mishnah. Five are the books of the Torah. Four are the matriarchs. Three are the patriarchs. Two are the tablets of the covenant. One is our G-d in Heaven and Earth.

Eliyahu Hanavi – The Prophet Elijah

אֵלִיָּהוּ הַנָּבִיא, אֵלִיָּהוּ הַתִּשְׁבִּי, אֵלִיָּהוּ הַגִּלְעָדִי, בִּמְהֵרָה יָבֹא אֵלֵינוּ עִם מָשִׁיחַ בֶּן דָּוִד.

Eliyahu ha-navi, Eliyahu ha-tishbi, Eliyahu ha-giladi. Bimheirah yavo eleynu, im Mashiach ben David.

May Elijah the prophet, Elijah the Tishbite, Elijah of Gilead, quickly in our day come to us heralding redemption with the Messiah, son of David.

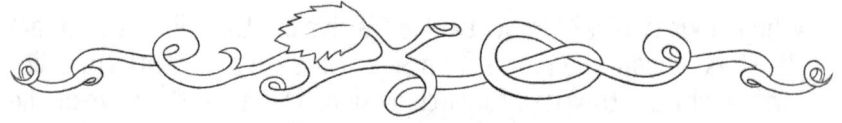

Let My People Go

"When Israel was in Egypt land, let my people go.
Oppressed so hard they could not stand, let my people go."
Go down, Moses, way down in Egypt land.
Tell old Pharaoh, let my people go!

"Thus saith the Lord" bold Moses said, "Let my people go,
If not I'll smite your firstborn dead, let my people go."
Go down, Moses, way down in Egypt land.
Tell old Pharaoh, let my people go!

"No more shall they in bondage toil, let my people go.
Let them come out with Egypt's spoils, let my people go."
Go down, Moses, way down in Egypt land.
Tell old Pharaoh, let my people go!

"When people stop this slavery, let my people go.
Soon may all the earth be free, let my people go."
Go down, Moses, way down in Egypt land.
Tell old Pharaoh, let my people go!

Appendix – Israeli Recipes

Tabbouleh Salad

Tabbouleh salad is a traditional Middle-Eastern side dish, popular in Israeli restaurants and households. Colorful and bursting with fresh vegetables and greens, it is a decorative addition to any festive table.

Ingredients (4-5 servings):

- 1.5 cups dry bulgur (or 1.5 cups quinoa, for a kosher for Passover alternative)
- 2 cups boiling water
- 0.5 cup chopped fresh parsley
- 0.45 cup chopped fresh mint leaves
- 3 large tomatoes
- 3 scallions
- 3 tbsp. olive oil
- Juice from 2 freshly squeezed lemons
- Salt & pepper to taste
- 0.5 cup pomegranate seeds (optional)

Instructions:

☞ Put the bulgur in a bowl with the boiling water and cover with a towel for 15 minutes until all the water has been absorbed. Separate gently with a fork.

☞ If substituting with quinoa for a kosher for Passover recipe, cook quinoa on low heat in 3 cups of water. Once cooked and cooled, separate gently with a fork.

☞ Dice the tomatoes small and chop the scallions. Add chopped parsley, mint leaves, tomatoes, and scallions to the bulgur or quinoa, once cool.

☞ In a separate bowl, mix olive oil, lemon juice, salt, and pepper to prepare the dressing.

☞ Dress and serve immediately.

☞ Optional – sprinkle pomegranate seeds for an extra pop of color and sweetness.

Charoset

The traditional Passover treat charoset is a mixture of apples, cinnamon, and walnuts that come together to create a sweet and symbolic dish, perfect for spreading on matzo or eating by the spoonful.

Ingredients (2 cups):

- 2 green apples
- 1 cup walnuts, chopped
- 1 tsp. ground cinnamon
- 0.25 cup sweet red wine
- 2 tbsp. honey
- 1 tbsp. freshly squeezed lemon juice
- Dates, almonds, or figs (optional)

Instructions:

- Core, peel, and dice the apples finely. Place in a mixing bowl. Add the chopped walnuts, ground cinnamon, red wine, honey, and lemon juice to the bowl and mix until well combined.

- Taste and adjust the flavors, adding honey, cinnamon, or lemon as needed.

- Chill for at least an hour before serving.

- Finely chop dates, almonds, or figs as desired and sprinkle over the charoset before serving.

Matzo-Ball Soup

Matzo-ball soup is the quintessential Jewish comfort food. Light and delicious, the stock combines flavors of chicken and vegetables and the matzo-balls add a nostalgic touch. No Passover is complete without it!

Ingredients (6-8 servings):

For the soup:

- 4 celery stalks
- Fresh parsley
- 2 carrots, halved
- 2 medium onions, halved
- 4 cloves of garlic, whole
- 4 whole chicken thighs
- 3 liters water
- Salt & pepper to taste

For the matzo balls:

- 1 cup matzo meal
- 1 tsp. baking powder
- 1 tsp. salt
- 2 tbsp. oil
- 1.5 cups boiling water
- 2 large eggs

Instructions:

- Put the celery, parsley, carrots, onions, garlic, and chicken in a large pot, cover with water, and bring to a boil. Add salt and pepper and allow to simmer for 2-3 hours, stirring and adding water as needed.

- Strain the chicken stock into another pot. You can cut the chicken and vegetables into smaller pieces and add them to the pot or leave the stock clear as it is.

☞ In a bowl, mix matzo meal, baking powder, salt, pepper, and oil. Add the boiling water and mix until combined. Cover and place in the fridge for 10 minutes. In a separate bowl, whisk the eggs.

☞ In a small pot, boil 2 liters of water with some salt. Remove the matzo ball mixture from the fridge and combine with the whisked eggs. Then, with wet hands, shape into matzo balls of your desired size. Place the balls gently in the boiling water and cook for 5-8 minutes on a low flame.

☞ Heat the soup before serving and add the matzo balls to warm for several minutes. Serve and enjoy!

Eggplant & Tahini Dip

This Middle-Eastern version of baba ganoush is smooth and tangy and pairs great with matzo!

Ingredients (4 servings):

- 2 whole eggplants
- 0.25 cup of raw tahini
- 2-3 cloves of garlic, crushed
- 2 tbsp. lemon juice
- Salt & pepper to taste
- Olive oil and parsley for garnishing

Instructions:

- Lightly stab all over the eggplants with a fork, then grill them whole at 420° for 40-45 minutes until they are scorched and soft.

- Let the eggplants cool before cutting them open and scraping out the light-colored meat inside. Let the filling rest in a strainer for 20-30 minutes until any spare liquids have been removed.

- Chop the eggplant finely and add it to a bowl with the tahini, garlic, lemon juice, and seasoning.

- Garnish with olive oil and chopped parsley.

Iced Limonana

Iced limonana (lemon and mint) is a classic Israeli drink to be found in any Tel Aviv café. Cold, sweet, and refreshing, it is the perfect drink for a hot Israeli summer day!

To order in Israel, ask for "limonana garus".

Ingredients (4-5 servings):

- 8 tbsp. sugar
- 0.5 cup boiling water
- 1.5 cups ice
- 1 cup fresh mint leaves
- 2 cups cold water
- Juice from 5 freshly squeezed lemons

Instructions:

- Stir the sugar into the boiling water until fully dissolved, then set aside.
- In a blender, blend the rest of the ingredients well – ice, mint, water, and lemon juice.
- Add the sugar water and mix thoroughly.
- Serve ice-cold and decorate with a slice of lemon and a sprig of mint leaves.

www.ingramcontent.com/pod-product-compliance
Lightning Source LLC
LaVergne TN
LVHW020429070526
838199LV00004B/338